THE ENCOURAGING EQUESTRIAN

A collection of *devotionals*
that apply to all walks and disciplines in life

JESSICA SHIVELY

The Encouraging Equestrian

Trilogy Christian Publishers A Wholly Owned Subsidiary of Trinity Broadcasting Network

2442 Michelle Drive Tustin, CA 92780

Trilogy Christian Publishing/TBN and colophon are trademarks of Trinity Broadcasting Network.

Cover design by: Kelly Stewart

For information about special discounts for bulk purchases, please contact Trilogy Christian Publishing.

10 9 8 7 6 5 4 3 2 1

Library of Congress Cataloging-in-Publication Data is available.

ISBN: 979-8-89041-083-2

E-ISBN: 979-8-89041-084-9

DEDICATION

To my grandpa who raised me. You showed me the love of horses and, most importantly, the love of my Father, Jesus Christ. When my earthly father was absent, you stepped in and never gave up on me. Thank you for always being the perfect mix of Jesus and John Wayne. I know you are smiling down from heaven.

To my husband—for growing my faith and pushing me to write. Thank you for being my cattle prod to take this leap in sharing my love of Christ with others. I love you more than you know.

TABLE OF CONTENTS

Unique in His Image

A horse is uniquely made in His Father's eyes. He gives each horse different attributes and "horsenalities," just as He created us with varying personalities and purpose.

The Lord established the ability of the horse long ago, engrained their natural instincts, to show His great power and grace, never wavering in trouble, but only to react the same, either fight or flight.

As humans, the Lord has uniquely made us all in His own image, giving us each our own identities in Christ. When we choose to live by His words, fully embracing His instructions of scriptures, we, too, can respond consistently, as a horse does, to fight or flee in situations we're put in. We are to fight the good fight and flee from temptation. Instead of responding out of emotion or speaking from our flesh, we must speak to the evil one with the wise words of Jesus Christ, for that is the name even demons tremble at.

We must seek completely after Jesus, filling our spirit with His guidance and building our foundation constantly through His leadership.

As a horse trainer, I ask each equine questions to see what they are capable of. I put them in positions of pressure to see how they react. I don't push them hard to the point of exploding. I guide each horse to a position of challenge to obtain a 1 percent increase. I prove to them in uncomfortable situations, I can be a worthy leader.

Unlike me, the Lord doesn't have to prove He is a worthy leader. He continues to pour out and show up in all our circumstances. He puts us in positions of pressure to grow and change us in Him. He willingly shows us that He is worthy and consistent. He never flees in doubt, like a horse or human can. He is always fighting for us, no matter how unqualified we may feel. The Lord knows we are capable, never pushing us to the point of explosion. He has a unique purpose for us and everyone else who is willing to embrace Him. Jesus never leaves us or forsakes us, and He is holding our hand through it all.

A dorsal stripe is a thin, narrow stripe running atop the widest part of the horse's back.

> For wide is the gate and broad is the road that leads to destruction, and many enter through it. But small is the gate and narrow the road that leads to life, and only few find it.

MATTHEW 7:13-14

We must strive to stay on that narrow path of everlasting love and faith in Christ Jesus.

Please and Thank You

Being kind and giving thanks is a necessary contribution when training horses, especially wildlies and stallions. Nothing is gained by initially demanding. When I train horses, I often share with folks that everything is done in phases. I ask, tell, then demand. I allow periods of waiting to allow the horse time to offer a try. I do my best to make the right things easy and the wrong things hard.

Think of it this way: You wouldn't yell at your husband to change the oil in your truck or scream at your kiddo to clean their room the first time around, would you? First, we ask out of kindness and love. Then go through the proper phases to achieve the pending request while keeping kindness and love attached. I'm not talking about being nice and polite. I'm talking about being kind.

Anyone can be nice and not care. Anyone can be polite, saying all the right things, but not have any heart in it. Anyone can offer one-time advice and have no desire to speak to you again. Anyone can say please without being sincere. Don't just give a care. Give your heart. When the heart is in it, that is true kindness.

Once the request is filled, offer praises with thankfulness.

Whether in life or in horsemanship, your kindness should be inspiring. In horses, kindness creates curiosity, which is fundamental in building a proper foundation. I offer the opportunity to try new things that build confidence with boundaries. When any horse I work with offers the slightest try, I reward it. I reward with thankfulness in lots of rubs and scratches of affirmation. The horse is affirmed with a powerful release and acts of kindness, not just empty words of niceness. I give the Lord thanks for listening to my every prayer and for all His help every minute of every day in my journey of salvation. This goodness overflows into horsemanship. Be thankful today. Don't forget your pleases and thank yous. Kindness goes out of the way, seeking no recognition. Be an example of selflessness. Don't just be nice, be kind.

> Praise the Lord. Give thanks to the Lord, for he is good; his love endures forever.
>
> PSALM 106:1

> A kindhearted woman gains honor, but ruthless men gain only wealth.
> Those who are kind benefit themselves, but the cruel bring ruin on themselves.
>
> PROVERBS 11:16-17

> *Every act of kindness and compassion done by any man for his fellow Christian is done by Christ working within him.*
>
> JULIAN OF NORWICH

Brand Ambassador

Our world today is constantly persuading us with the wrong information. Our world today pushes false gods, fake news, lies built on lies, confusion built on the devil's schemes, and an idea of dictatorship of what to believe, what to buy, and how to live. All these things are available to cause confusion and delusion, drawing folks away from the truth and light found in Jesus Christ.

Some folks are too concerned about making a name for themselves. Some folks are too concerned about sporting the most famous names. These are misconceptions of the devil. The devil came to kill, steal, and destroy. He loves to distract us from the goodness of Jesus with fake shining and sparkling things. The devil loves to draw our attention to focus on self—versus selflessness found in Christ. The devil loves to expand pride in what is seen instead of what is unseen. He loves to point out our sins, leading to a pit of condemnation.

But God!

God made His Son, who had no sin to be sin for us, so that in Him, we might become the righteous of God. May we be Ambassadors of God's love, not advertise the lies of the devil.

Whether in life or in horsemanship, there are many

great brands available to us, from equipment to clothes, to boots, to food. Do not get distracted by false religions, false teachers, and fancy brands. These things do not define us, nor should we let them. Brands are JUST RESOURCES, not the source. The greatest brand to advertise that the world so desperately needs is the brand of Jesus. He is THE SOURCE.

I challenge you today, instead of focusing on readily available brands on the radio, billboards, phone screens, computer screens, etc. How about focusing on the character and love of Jesus? How about being a readily available resource of Jesus? How about being a brand Ambassador of God's love? When we find ourselves fully relying on Christ, He's renewing us, changing us for the good, giving us an overflow of peace, and giving us an opportunity to excel in Him. No number of worldly brands will give us peace like the brand of Jesus. He's giving us an opportunity to come to Him, to be renewed, to have a new life, and advertise His love and grace for as long as we keep Him in our lives. We must be willing to keep the Lord's word in our hearts, follow His truth, and stay focused on His goodness. For Jesus is the way, the truth, and the life. The One and Only True God, no lies, no confusion, and no distractions by shining and sparkling things.

> We are therefore Christ's ambassadors, as though God were making His appeal through us. We implore you on Christ's behalf: Be reconciled to God.
>
> 2 CORINTHIANS 5:20

There's a Difference

There's a difference between hearing and listening.

There's a difference between change and excuses.

There's a difference in reading and understanding.

There's a difference between emotion and guidance by the Holy Spirit.

There's a difference between love and lust.

There's a difference between hope and faith.

There's a difference between greed and gratitude.

There's a difference between giving out of kindness versus for recognition.

There's a difference between leadership and dictatorship.

There's a difference between cowboys versus cowboyin'.

There's a difference between horsemanship built on world views versus horsemanship built on a right relationship.

There's a difference between religion versus having a right relationship with Christ.

There's a difference between judging and inspecting fruits.

There's a difference between condemnation and conviction.

There's a difference between insult and loving correction.

There's a difference between telling and teaching.

There's a difference between knowing about Jesus versus knowing Him.

Don't allow your circumstances, your dry season, unpleasant people, and challenges to change you. Allow Christ to change you.

Many of these differences get muddled quickly with a selfish outlook based on secular conclusions.

Only Christ can give you clarity for truth.

There's a big difference.

> But seek first his kingdom and his righteousness, and all these things will be given to you as well.
>
> MATTHEW 6:33

Beware of Wolves in
Sheep's Clothing

Some people have our best interest at heart. Some people just want to take our money. In a world today that promotes self, be cautious of those who claim to help you. Be vigilant of those folks who want to help but then expect something in return. It's far better to give than receive. Be mindful of the folks who want quick fixes or results instantly. We live in a fast-food world, but not all things of value are obtainable from a drive-thru window. Services of value and good ethics that reflect the fruits of the spirit, wisdom, and truth require effort on our behalf. We must be willing to research character and see if the results align with the truth of the gospel. When we don't put effort in or ask the Lord for clarity, the truth will not be revealed.

Whether in life or in horsemanship, it's absolutely disgusting the number of people that fool consumers and clients with types of services offered. Not all are qualified to lead and teach. It's up to us to put forth effort, do research, and pray for discernment. Now I'm not talking about "research" from the platform of Google. Not all things available on the web are true. Wikipedia can be modified, articles are typically one-sided, and forums are based on one's resolution. Inspect fruits that are barred from such services offered. Be involved in the training and teachings. Growth can't be achieved at a distance. If something doesn't make sense, ask questions directly to the source being used. If things are being forced instead of willingly presented, a right relationship is never established. Be vigilant to not be fooled by wolves in sheep's clothing. For the devil prowls around, waiting to seek, devour, and destroy. But God!

Jesus will reveal the truth. He will reveal false teachers and trainers. He will reveal the falsehood of evil spirits. Stay rooted in Jesus' word for guidance, knowledge, and wisdom to discern good and evil, uneducated versus educated, and opinions versus truth. Beware of the curtain of confusion. Allow the Lord to lift the veil for clearer vision. For Jesus is the Ultimate Trainer, and He can guide you through the arena of life. Test the spirits and pray for direction and discernment.

> Dear friends, do not believe every spirit, but test the spirits to see whether they are from God, because many false prophets have gone out into the world.
>
> 1 JOHN 4:1

Walk Your Talk

True wisdom is not necessarily found in those with the most education, money, or friends. Rather, wise people can be spotted living wisely in humility, participating in good works, enjoying peace, singleness of purpose, and gentle lifestyles.

Words and actions should reflect one another. If they don't, don't be a fool and ignore it. Be aware of the deception. You should be able to walk your talk, not one or the other.

Whether in life or in horsemanship, it should be evident in your actions of the understanding of the right relationship with Jesus or a horse. There are many false teachers and false trainers. There are plenty that start teaching the gospel or advertise to start young mustangs and horses without having the proper knowledge to do so. Make sure you inspect their fruits. Evaluate the teacher's character and evaluate previous horses trained.

Do not slander those that falsely advertise themselves but go to the Lord in prayer for the lies to be revealed. When you take on the title of being a teacher, you will be judged more strictly. So, make sure the Lord has prepared you. Don't step out of His will, and make sure that you teach what is right. Don't just muddy your way through it and accept money without doing the work right. To be effective, you must have true understanding, knowledge, and the Lord's wisdom. For His teachings are the way, the truth, and the life. For real faith shows itself through deeds. To be successful, you must be consistent every... single... day.

> In the same way, faith by itself if it is not accompanied by action, is dead.

JAMES 2:17

Stewards of the Lord's Creation

God calls us to be stewards or trustees of His creation. A great example: animals. The Bible reminds us that we are responsible to Him for the way we treat them. God gave humans dominion over animals to use them for work and recreation. Not by any means to abuse them or defile them.

Animals serve a higher purpose than being locked in a cage or fenced off in an area less than they deserve. Animals are a gift from God, a privilege to own. Humans are charged with compassion to learn from an animal's humility. It takes proper faith and a right relationship with Christ to correctly care for them. God has compassion and love toward animals. He provides everything needed for them, just as He provides everything needed for us. All we must do is trust Him. Unfortunately, animals don't have the choice to pick their owners, so don't make their life miserable. Show Christ even in your relationship with your animal. Provide everything necessary for them just as God does for us. How you take care of your animal shows the value of your integrity. Be mindful of the commitment of time and money when considering adding a furry pet to your family. We must look past "free to good home" or a cheap adoption fee. Whether in life or horsemanship, if it's a puppy, a cat, a foal, or a horse, pray about it first.

A righteous man cares for the needs of his animal, but the kindest acts of the wicked are cruel.

PROVERBS 12:10

People often forget the real responsibility of taking care of God's creations. When you hurt God's creation, you are also hurting yourself.

Give them life they deserve. Give them love and purpose, just as Christ does for us.

Are You a Fruitful Branch
or a Barren Stick?

A friendly correction can come off as humiliating someone you see as competition. Social media shouldn't be a platform to argue or point out wrongs or faults but should be a place to encourage and uplift one another in Christ. Facebook, Instagram, TikTok, Twitter, etc., make it easy to bully people from a distance and influence those around us negatively. Trash is easily accessible through these platforms right at our fingertips. All the media exploited is a way to hide the truth and escape the consequences of the real world.

If a correction is coming from a place of love and humility, do so in private. If it isn't, keep your mouth shut.

Whether in life or in horsemanship, not all are qualified to teach, plant seeds, correct, or rebuke. There are so many teachers that are ill-equipped to share knowledge. Most are sharing opinions. Most are not physically and mentally fit to handle the truth. Then when faced with challenges, the circumstances end up changing the person rather than Christ changing them.

They're missing the pruning from Jesus to be effective teachers in Christ. Now we all fall short of the glory, but if we are not continually changing for the better or turning away from sin, we're missing the importance of salvation.

The Lord will expose our motives, our intentions, and the people we are connected too. The fruits bear will reveal what type of branch we are. May we be a person who remains in Jesus, bearing much fruit. If we are a barren stick, apart from Jesus, we are easily tossed into the fire. We are nothing without Jesus, for Jesus is the true vine.

Whether horse or human, may we correct from a place of humility, not disgrace. May we cultivate fruits of the Spirit. May we allow the true Gardener to clean us up, prune us, and grow us to be fruitful. He will guide us to ways of fruition. But we must stay in Him to bear such fruit.

For He is the way, the truth, and the life. He is the foundation of the right relationship. He is the Ultimate Trainer, the most knowledgeable Teacher, and the Greatest Gardner.

> I am the true vine, and my Father is the gardener. He cuts off every branch in me that bears no fruit, while every branch that does bear fruit he prunes so that it will be even more fruitful. You are already clean because of the word I have spoken to you. Remain in me, and I will remain in you. No branch can bear fruit by itself; it must remain in the vine. Neither can you bear fruit unless you remain in me. I am the vine; you are the branches. If a man remains in me and I in him, he will bear much fruit; apart from me you can do nothing.

> JOHN 15:1–5

Valor, a Wild Filly That Stole My Heart

BLM Freezebrand #: ****8313
Rounded up from Antelope Valley, Nevada

The sighs and snickers filled the backdrop as I backed up my 30' gooseneck rig. Some folks see a shiny white truck, my bright pink hair, a petite young gal, and go to judgin', thinking I don't have a clue as to what I'm doing. It may be legit, or it may all be in my head. As people say, we are our worst critics. Little do they know, I'm prior service, a Marine Corps veteran, and was a motor transportation operator. I've been teaching and training in the horse industry for over twenty years. After a hurricane years ago hit my town in North Carolina, I was blessed with the opportunity to adopt two mustangs with baggage. After restarting these mustangs, also known as wildlies, these horses blew in a fresh wind to work with wild horses. I, too, dreamed the dream many have of slipping off that neck tag charm. Fast forward a few years... And a few tedious months, I finally received my approval as a trainer through the Bureau of Land Management (BLM) and the Mustang Heritage Foundation (MHF).

Completely last minute, I made my way to a pickup location in Georgia. I took the leap and listened to the encouraging words of friends and other mustang owners.

The environment was inviting, friendly, and chattering as I stepped out of my truck into a new scene of the un-gentled mustang world. Much like how my fresh boots hit the sand in the desert of Iraq. I was nervous, excited, and possibly too chatty. I watched as some fabulous ladies loaded my two yearlings. One I adopted out, and the other I adopted for a Trainer Challenge. After getting home and settled, morning came, and I worked with my mustang #8313 for a few minutes. Later that afternoon, she braved and approached me, reaching out her nose to sniff me, nudge me, and came closer for the overwhelming first tag-off feeling. I believe in the power of names, and the Lord has laid a charge on my heart to name my mustangs with purpose. The Lord spoke to me through one of my favorite scriptures, Joshua 1:9, leading me to her name, Valor. She's strong and courageous and has taught me much, as many horses do. I ended up keeping her after the Trainer Challenge. She's, of course, one of my personal horses, who I also use in my riding program and Mustang and Veteran program: Operation No Longer a Number. Valor has sealed my love of working with mustangs, as we can all come from a wild place in need of gentling. Valor has a way of growing courage in a person's soul regardless of conditions.

> Have I not commanded you? Be strong and courageous. Do not be terrified; do not be discouraged, for the Lord your God will be with you wherever you go.
>
> JOSHUA 1:9

Realistic Goals

The Bible is the most beloved and powerful book of all time. It was the first book ever published; it is translated into more languages than any other in history and remains the best seller of all best sellers. No book has enlightened so much darkness, educated so much ignorance, propagated so much love, reprimanded so much evil, or predicted the future so accurately as the Bible. It not only explains our origins and purpose for life but how we can know God here and in eternity beyond the grave. For some people, the Bible seems just too big to understand. They don't know where or how it all began. But as a Christian, you're not left alone to try to grasp the major themes and deep meaning of the Bible. The Holy Spirit, who now lives in your heart by the way of salvation, is an illuminator of Truth. His truth. It's not necessary or possible to understand the Lord's way and have trust and faith in Him that His Word doesn't come back void (Isaiah 55:8–11).

> The Spirit searches all things, even the deep things of God.
>
> 1 CORINTHIANS 2:10

And because of His internal lamp, the scriptures are now yours to read, absorb, comprehend, and live by.

But first, you've got to commit to doing it.

Be in the Word daily.

Stay in the Word.

Live the Word.

Be an example of Christ every day.

Do not strive for an unrealistic goal of perfection. Strive for a realistic goal of progression.

Be better than the day before.

Be humbled by your shortcomings and/or imperfections.

Embrace correction out of love.

Seek more of Christ and His attributes every chance you are given.

Extend grace to those you love, as well as the people and horses that rub you the wrong way.

Shine the Lord's internal light, which is the Holy Spirit living in you, and watch Him move those mountains in your path.

Don't Hinder a Weaker Brother or Sister

Oftentimes, we can get offended when someone more knowledgeable wants to share something with us. Sometimes, higher knowledge can come off as arrogance as the lack of humility isn't present. Instead of passing judgment as we are so quick to do, what if we decided to not be a stumbling block or a hindrance to others and ourselves? What if we decided not to respond with offense built upon selfish defense? What if we decided not to argue over silly opinions? What if we decided to keep our mouths shut and just listen to the advice? What if we decided to dress ourselves with humility to be open to higher knowledge? What if we decided to be open to learning from a source of truth, such as Jesus? Worldly mentorship is far different from being guided by Christ Jesus.

Whether in life or horsemanship, welcome those who have weak knowledge and faith. Don't quarrel over opinions. We must allow ourselves to be taught, to grow, and be challenged so we can change to be more Christ-like. Those who are in a position to be mentored pay attention to the fruits that are barred by who you're learning from. Test the spirits, seek discernment from Christ to illuminate truth. Make sure these mentors are starting with the basics, as not all are qualified to teach.

When I'm teaching a student for the first time, I do not pass judgment on what they know or don't know. We always start at the beginning of grooming our horse, getting some quality time in before we just hop on, just as I start from the beginning when I'm training a horse. I want to make sure I'm not hindering the relationship by jumping in the middle. A right relationship starts from the beginning: the foundation and belief that Christ died for my sins, was buried, and rose on the third day. Without basic understanding, greater concepts will not make sense.

When simplicity is mastered, each day, we can add stepping stones of wisdom. Growing the horse and human from weakness in ourselves to strength and reliance in Christ Jesus.

Just as the Lord mentors us with humility, we must also do the same. Jesus laid Himself down. He made Himself lower in position to effectively minister to our hearts. We must decrease so Jesus can increase. Welcome your weaker brother and sisters. Seek truth and correct mentorship. Be willing to listen. Don't be a stumbling block to others but be a stepping stone. Be open to a lifelong commitment of change and blessings. Those who are strong ought to bear with the failings of the weak. Each of us should take a little time to build others up. Don't be a people pleaser, be a Jesus pleaser. Seeking His words daily to point others to hope in Jesus. Don't be a salty heifer, be salt of the earth, keeping its flavor. Minister to the horse and human in front of you, keep it simple, start with the basics, and allow the Lord to grow you from there. For He is the way, the truth, and the life.

> Therefore let us stop passing judgement on one another. Instead, make up your mind not to put any stumbling block or obstacle in your brothers way.

> ROMANS 14:13

Focus on the Now,
Not the End Goal

No one has ever found a limit to what the horse–human partnership can accomplish. Most of us lose our way by concentrating on the goal of task and not the depth of relationship. We narrow our focus, seeing only with tunnel vision. Are focus and commitment required to achieve goals? Absolutely. The issue is what we focus on and what goals we set. My point is that unnecessary limits on what is possible by focusing on goals using only our own intellect and vision. God's vision is limitless.

LYNN BABER

When we try to control every circumstance, we tend to make it worse. It causes more confusion and anxiety. If we allow to truly trust Jesus Christ with our life and set all our burdens on Him, He will guide us faithfully, without issues. His plan for us is limitless if we allow Him to steer us. Just as I'm working and training with horses. I build a relationship first. I don't focus on all the things the horse can or can't do. When I'm to the point, I can start teaching to steer. I start by applying very little pressure; I correct what's needed, not everything at once. I allow for mistakes. I focus on our relationship now, not the end goal at first.

If too much pressure is applied, whether it's with legs, seat, or reins, it confuses the horse. We humans love to have a sense of control and often micromanage. We then love to overcomplicate things leading us to over steer, grip with our booty, knees, and use additional pressure to try to fix it. All of this leads to getting in the horse's way.

You must allow them to guide you, light and right.

Don't narrow their knowledge. Horses already know how to turn left, right, roll back, slide, stop, cut, and jump. It's up to us to allow them to do it without getting in their way with lack of confidence and control. We must learn how to speak to them just as we must learn to speak to Christ.

Jesus Christ is always there; He's always waiting for that extended hand to be a helper. He craves a relationship with us just as a horse craves one with its trusted leader. Let all your dreams and worries rest on Him. Don't let yourself limit Christ's expectations for you. Don't add additional pressure and get in the Lord's way.

Abandon everything to Christ. Abandonment to God offers true blessings of insight and experiences that aren't possible by any other means. Let Him be in control.

The Lord is my light and salvation—whom shall I fear?

PSALM 27:1

He will provide you strength, the deepest security, and personal safety.

Have a Student
Frame of Mind

The good news of Jesus Christ and the fundamentals of Natural Horsemanship have been around since the beginning of time. There are so many people who are oblivious to both truths. What makes these topics so new and interesting for people who are unaware of both?

I believe it's, in fact, how they hear the message. Jesus did not reinvent the wheel, so to speak, of His Father's will, hope, and love for all people in finding salvation through Him.

Just as Tom Dorrance, Ray Hunt, Buck Brannaman, Monty Roberts, and Pat Parelli didn't reinvent the wheel in teaching Natural Horsemanship.

These fancy, publicly known figures really should be known for not being horse whisperers but for seeing themselves as less. They humbly pride themselves on being a student of the horse. All these trainers have one thing in common: True understanding of the relationship.

Just as Jesus understands the importance of having a relationship with Him, His Father, and the Holy Spirit. The Lord humbly laid Himself down for all our transgressions so that we can willingly come to Jesus at any time, not just as a student but as a son and daughter.

Whether in life or in horsemanship, don't be fooled by all the different trainers and religions available. See through the smoke, lights, and fancy tricks. Ask yourself, what fruits are being barred? Is it evident that things are forced? Or are they willing?

Are they creating a robotic horse? Or a willing partner?

Does your horse run to you? Or does it run from you? Are they going through the motions of a training DVD with no understanding of what and why? Are they going through the motions of religious practices just because that's what everyone else does?

When you have a true understanding of the relationship, meaning a personal partnership, you then will be enlightened to the details. Have a humble frame of mind to be a student of the Lord and a student of the horse.

Always be willing to learn. Don't reinvent the wheel, as that dilutes foundational truth. Don't add to or take away from the truth. Be sensitive in a hard-pressed world that glorifies evil. Don't let this world or your experiences numb you to truth, love, and grace.

In my horsemanship, I always strive to leave my horses in a peaceful frame of mind. I want to leave them to where they seek me and our right relationship. Leading them to run to me instead of running from me.

Just as the Lord wants to offer peace, love, grace, strength, forgiveness, and goodness every time when we willingly run to Him.

Come to me, all you who are weary and burdened, and I will give you rest. Take my yoke upon you and learn from me, for I am gentle and humble in heart, and you will find rest for your souls. For my yoke is easy and my burden is light.

MATTHEW 11:28-30

A Few Reminders

Instead of focusing on a failing world, focus on an unfailing God.

Instead of making a change in other countries, focus on the area around you that needs change.

Instead of giving thousands of dollars away to stocks, government organizations, hate groups, and crimes, rightfully give and tithe your dollars to the One and Only King Jesus who blesses you. Put that money back into HIS ministries!

Instead of raising a lawless generation being mentored by social media, Hollywood TV, and video games, start raising your children with godly influence.

Instead of whining and complaining about how high things are getting and how expensive gas, clothes, and groceries are, start complaining and PRAYING to Jesus!

One of the biggest issues today is the rebellion of people trying to do their own thing and disregarding the Lord Jesus' words of wisdom. The Bible is a crucial guide to read to help you navigate this life successfully. It is Basic Instructions Before Leaving Earth. If you want a short life as a result of damnation, go ahead and keep living your life the way YOU want to.

A wiser option: stop living like the world sees fit. Live a life where the Lord Jesus is the head of it. He offers fulfillment, peace, joy, direction, release from depression, oppression, anxiety, and drama!

Now I'm not saying your walk with the Lord will be easy, but the result is far better than hell. So, wake up! Oh, sleepers! Focus on an unfailing Jesus. Always be looking for His return because He is coming back! For He is the way, the truth, and the life, and the Lord Jesus will give you hope in a lost generation.

> Gather together, yes, gather, O shameless nation, before the decree takes effect—before the day passes away like chaff—before there comes upon you the burning anger of the Lord, before there comes upon you the day of the anger of the Lord. Seek the Lord, all you humble of the land, who do his just commands; seek righteousness; seek humility; perhaps you may be hidden on the day of the anger of the Lord.

> ZEPHANIAH 2:2-3

Skilled Work

Proverbs 23:29 reminds us, "Do you see a man skilled in his work? He will stand before kings; he will not stand before obscure men." Scripture doesn't simply qualify this statement, and neither do people. Faith and works go hand in hand. You can't have one without the other.

If you are skilled at whatever you do, you will stand, or you will have a place to stand before kings. We might not have the opportunity to stand in the presence of an earthly king, but someday we will all stand before the King. The Lord's Word teaches us that He is concerned with how well we do the work that He has given us to do.

Whether in life or in horsemanship, there's more to it than what appears at face value. A horse is more than just a pretty face, just as scripture is more than just words printed in a book.

There's an underlying meaning, like an onion. There are many layers to peel back to unveil the true stinging meaning of truths that will be revealed from Christ. We just have to be willing to listen.

When we build the right relationship with Jesus, we will have an open line of communication, whether in prayer or when we seek Him out in scripture. It's not about our assumptions. It's about what He reveals to us.

When I work with horses, whether my own or ones in training, I establish the right relationship first, built on trust, confidence, and security. I do not hold grudges, and I do not assume anything based on general looks or false knowledge. A horse is a horse. They reveal your good or bad intentions. They tattle-tale on our inconsistencies. They detect shallowness, and they reveal what flows from our hearts. They reveal the deepest emotions, whether we like it or not.

We get what we give.

If you want more from both your horse and Jesus, get deeper, become more rooted, grow in knowledge, and become fully committed.

Jesus is always Jesus. He is constant. He is the truth. He provides security if you allow yourself to be guided by Him. He doesn't match our good deeds like a 401k. He's not a blessing vending machine. He's not wishy-washy, He doesn't hold grudges, and He's not waiting for you to be perfect to come to Him.

He wants to love you completely.

He's after your heart, but it's up to you to surrender to His goodness.

How well are you doing the job that the Lord has given you to do? No matter if you are a farmer, a horse trainer, a butcher, a baker, a candlestick maker, a barista, etc.... we are to work according to Colossians 3:17, "And whatever you do, whether in word or deed, do it all in the name of the Lord Jesus, giving thanks to God the Father through him."

As men and women, we were created to honor God in our work, no matter what position He has blessed us with.

Be Coachable

When we run out of knowledge, we often punish our horses.

Don't be haughty, be humble in what you know and what you don't know.

Every professional athlete has a coach and trainer. That means you are not exempt either. Unless you are fine with being a survival rider. However, there's more to riding than just surviving. You're missing out on a fabulous, rewarding relationship where you can help grow your horse. However, you must be willing to be coachable. It is hard to progress in riding and training alone. You will eventually find yourself doing the same thing over and over, making zero progress, getting thrown off, stomped on, discouraged, angry, and spinning around like dust bunnies sucked up in your vacuum.

Whether in faith or in horsemanship, surround yourself with like-minded folks. Fellowship with those who will push you, grow you, build you up, and aren't afraid to correct you in love. Have mentors who are qualified in their teachings in and out of the arena.

If you're not learning or feeling a sense of correction

from conviction, you're not growing. Those who think they know everything will be the death of themselves. Do not be conceited, envious, or provoking of one another. Do not compare yourself to someone else, for the Lord made you in His own image with a purpose in mind. But you must be willing to seek after Him, grow in Him, and share His love and grace so you can become equipped for every good work.

> All Scripture is God-breathed and is useful for teaching, rebuking, correcting and training in righteousness, so that the servant of God may be thoroughly equipped for every good work.
>
> 2 TIMOTHY 3:16-17

Be All in or Nothing

Whether in life or horsemanship, we will get the best results by fully committing. When we have wishy-washy faith and horsemanship, we are setting an example of fence-sitting. We can't be trained to our full potential if we are clinging to the corral panels. When we overextend ourselves, we will find ourselves in a black hole of depression and exhaustion. We can't make progress by fleeing in times of trouble. We must be willing to get uncomfortable to grow. The Lord exposes those who puff up themselves, as does a horse.

If you're not humble enough to learn, you're on a fast track to getting hurt.

We will never be able to steward a human or a horse to the best of our ability, living outside of the Lord's will.

We must be willing to lay ourselves down and pick up His cross daily. The Lord isn't interested in our intelligence but in our instincts. The instinct of knowing there's more to life than following worldly concepts. Stop running around in circles in the round pen of life. Think of others first before yourself. Allow the Lord to work in your life and in your heart. Knowing scripture and sharing

scripture are two very different things, just as knowing OF
Christ and having a personal relationship with Christ are
widely different.

Apply ALL the Lord's scripture and seek Jesus daily.
For the Lord Jesus will fill that emptiness inside you
and give you purpose. We live in a world that has an evil
agenda to strike disaccord between people. The world
wants people to tear down each other, compete with one
another, talk trash about one another, and promote evil
plots of dragging folks down to failure. But God! Those
who have Christ in them are a light to this fallen world.
I want you to see that Jesus' light in me. May you find
success and joy. May the Lord get a hold of your mind
and your tongue and do wonders to change the perversion
coming out of it to words of encouragement and life. For
you can only be drawn by the Spirit. I pray the Holy Spirit
draws you, just as my horses are drawn to me. No strings
attached. No bribes or motives, just plain natural instincts.
Be all in. As you are considerate of the entire horse, you
must consider and apply the whole Bible.

> But seek first his kingdom and his righteousness, and
> all these things will be given to you as well.

MATTHEW 6:33

God-fidence,
the True Essence
of Confidence

The standard dictionary definition of confidence is to have the feeling or belief that one can rely on someone or something: firm trust.

Instead of having a willy-nilly version of self-confidence, be who Christ called you to be. Stand firm and have God-fidence. It's truth in knowing you can't do this life alone, but HE can. Put your faith and trust in Christ Jesus to lead you, provide for you, and change you. God-fidence is far from arrogance. Arrogance and self-pride overrun this world. Arrogance shines its light on self and illuminates pity, hate, jealousy, and a sense of competition. I'm faced with many girls, children, and adults that feel the need to compete with me. A subtle reminder—real women don't compete with one another. We lift one another up. We know this world is full of confusion, filth, and misleading information. Don't be fooled. Real women don't rely on themselves. We rely on the One and Only King Jesus. This is what sets us women apart from the girls. We have God-fidence, not a fake version of arrogance and self-fulfillment.

Girls who think they are better than you, know more than you, have better qualities or possessions than you, and have false hope in worldly lies. What to do in the meantime? Pray for them. Ask the Lord to change their hearts. Keep pouring Jesus into their lives indirectly or directly. We are not meant to fix our haters, neigh-sayers, or those who see us as competition. We are purposely placed in people's lives to share the good news, which is the love and light of Jesus. Whether in life or in horsemanship, it's most difficult to share Jesus with those who aren't our top fans, top hands, favorite horses, best students, mentees, or those who are willing to learn or be educated by us. But still, pour Jesus out. No excuses, no lies, no confusion, no competing with one another, just be real, and be who the Lord made you to be. You are a daughter and son of the Most High King. Your full potential will be revealed only in Christ Jesus.

Seal it with a K.I.S.S., Keep It Simple Stupid, y'all.

Stand firm on the Lord's Word, His character, and purpose. Move forward in God-fidence.

> Be anxious for nothing, but in everything, by prayer and petition, with thanksgiving, present your requests to God.
>
> PHILIPPIANS 4:6

Jesus Had
Neigh-Sayers Too

In this life on earth, you will be tested. You will have haters and neigh-sayers come against you. You will be falsely accused, you will be hurt, you will experience trials, you will be faced with false prophets, slander, and every other emotion under the sun. Jesus Christ is not the author of confusion. He is confidence, assurance, and humility, and will expose ALL darkness in any situation you face. The pain you will feel will be real, but it is nothing compared to the pain Jesus felt dying for all our sins on the cross.

When you face sin and those who wish to drag your name in the dirt, remember this: Jesus was rejected too. Do not avenge or retaliate. Commit the situation 110 percent to Jesus, and have quiet integrity. Sometimes, gently confronting the slanderer does no good, as those who have reprobate minds think they do nothing wrong. You can't reason with a fool, but the Lord can! It's best to be silent and allow the Lord to justify you and expose the sin, not you. Having sure confidence in the gospel reduces our fleshly reaction to being defensive. The flesh wants to seek to restore our worldly reputation, but really, we should remember that Christ's reputation is far greater than our own. The Lord always intercedes on our behalf. He will not let us drown. He will vindicate us. It may not be instant, but the Lord always exposes darkness. Allow Him to fight your battles. He has far better victory over it than we do. Trust Him to care for you and sustain you.

Whatever storm you are facing today, have rest, peace, and assurance that Jesus Christ will make a way when there seems to be no way.

Whether in life or in horsemanship, don't wallow and celebrate in a pity party, for great things never come easy. If you're not being attacked by the fiery darts of the devil, then you're living out a shallow relationship with Jesus. If you're not being tested, you're not learning or being molded into a better reflection of Jesus. If you're not being challenged by sin, you won't learn how to fight arrogance, hate, pride, and selfishness properly with Jesus.

When you live a life for Jesus, people will come against you. They will be jealous of you. Haters will confront you and feel the need to prove themselves to you by falsely claiming they're the next best thing, they know it all, and that they're better than you.

Look past the wolf in sheep's clothing, for without Jesus, we are nothing, and so are the haters. Those who feel the need to prove themselves, they are insecure and unwise. When folks are falsely grounded in confusion and false gods, motivated by evil talk, jealousy, arrogance, and laziness, they're sealing their fate in a lake of fire and torment.

In life and in horsemanship, be vulnerable to experience fullness, love, and joy, and be transformed by profound holy teachings by the One and Only King Jesus. Read His Word and remind yourself of it often. Be considerate of others, and don't take their hurtful words or looks to heart, for they are battling their own personal demons. Folks who try to defame others are typically guilty of the sin there trying to point out. They find satisfaction in bullying others, thinking selfishly higher of themselves. They have hope in things in a lost world, and they need prayer just as much as everyone else does. Kill the devils all around with Jesus' grace, love, and kindness.

For only hope, peace, love, and joy can be found in Jesus. It cannot be found in Confucius, Gandhi, the Virgin Mary, the Islamic Allah, or any other false gods, ONLY in Jesus Christ. Eternal life is only found in the One True King, King Jesus. So, don't let the devil dim your Jesus' light. Keep shining, smiling, and speaking of the hope that is found in Jesus.

> For He is the way, the truth, and the life. Jesus answered, "I am the way and the truth and the life. No one comes to the Father except through me."
>
> JOHN 14:6

Interruptions
or Invitations

True productivity isn't about tightly controlling ourselves and our calendars but about unleashing ourselves in love towards others. As Matt Perman observes, "All productivity practices, all of our work, everything is given to us by God for the purpose of serving others." If we view our work in isolation from others, and a potential interruption must be avoided at all costs, we're probably functioning out of a wrong motivation and certainly operating under faulty assumptions about the purpose of work.

When we place our thoughts, the day's plans, and agenda over others, we miss the truth of Christ standing right in front of us. Interruptions can seem inconvenient. When we have the right relationship with Christ and our minds aren't blocked by our emotions, a selfish attitude, or a woe-me attitude, our perspective will change.

We should see interruptions as an invitation of opportunity from Christ to get us back on track.

Interruptions make us stop what we are doing and adjust. We shouldn't adjust to a situation on our own will and strength. When we do, it will surely lead to failure. If we remember to rely on Jesus in these circumstances, blessings will pour out from this invitation. We can't stay in the Lord's will with selfish motives, running from our callings in Christ, or staying confused, gripping to worldly things and values. What a gloomy life to live in such turmoil! Believing in anything and having hope in nothing. There is no hope in the things of the world, but there is hope and purpose in Jesus Christ. For He is the way, the truth, and the life.

Whether in life or in horsemanship, what's your perspective? Are you faced with an interruption or an invitation to be redirected?

Be still. Change your way of thinking. View your detours as a chance to pause, rethink, and reevaluate. For our ways and plans should never be above the horses and humans placed in our life. To properly steward, we must be humble to be led by the Ultimate Trainer. We must be willing to grow ourselves, which will filter into our works.

Listen and seek direction from the One and Only King Jesus. Allow the Lord to redirect you and make you better. Have a godly perspective instead of a worldly one. Your interruptions, detours, and bad luck are opportunities from the Lord. The Ultimate Trainer always gives us an invitation of opportunity to get back on the right path to trust in Him.

> "For my thoughts are not your thoughts, neither are your ways my ways," declares the Lord. "As the heavens are higher than the earth, so are my ways higher than your ways and my thoughts than your thoughts."

> ISAIAH 55:8-9

Willing Sacrifice

Today, the word "sacrifice" can seem to be a scary word. But for those who are saved and know Jesus, it's far from a cult-like definition. The biblical meaning of sacrifice is to give the Lord whatever He requires of our time, our earthly possessions, and our efforts to further His work, to glorify the kingdom of Jesus Christ.

The Lord commanded, "Seek ye first the kingdom of God, and his righteousness…" (Matthew 6:33a, KJV) Our willingness to sacrifice is an indication of our devotion to the Lord. It is death to our fleshly wants to receive our fulfillment and need in Christ. Now don't get all morbid on me, we are not literally killing ourselves or sacrificing our life for a person or that first ride, but it does take effort to disciple our flesh to stand firm against the devil's schemes. We must be willing to sacrifice in spirit, to offer ourselves wholeheartedly to live for Jesus. Jesus offered His life to wash all our sins so we could have a new life in Him.

Whether in life or in horsemanship, some moments feel like survival of the hunger games, but when doubt creeps in, don't be self-confident, tap into God-fidence. When you may think that the green colt isn't ready, but the Lord knows better. Rebuke the fear and know fear is a liar. Fear is of the enemy. When you're nervous about sharing a testimony, don't let anxiety overtake you. Sharing the light of Jesus may just save a soul.

Jesus paid the ultimate price by physically dying as a willing sacrifice. He left His helper, the Holy Spirit, to those who are willing to sacrifice to live for Him. For the Lord does not desire sacrifice but desires mercy. Be willing to act with justice, mercy, and humility, just like our Father.

> But go and learn what this means: "I desire mercy, not sacrifice. For I have not come to call the righteous, but sinners."
>
> MATTHEW 9:12-13

Act Justly, Love Mercy, and Walk Humbly

Simple words don't have clear meanings as they used to. It's insane to think when searching for a definition of a word, you must be specific to find out the truth. You must decipher from the urban dictionary worldly dictionary, Webster, Wikipedia, etc. Instead, let's avoid confusion and seek out foundational truth, such as the everlasting, never-changing biblical definition of words. Those have clarity and value.

Let's take a gander at the word "humility." It comes from the Latin word *humilis* (low, slight), compare to Greek χαμαλός (khamalós, "on the ground, low, trifling"). Pay close attention to the translation of the word "low." Oftentimes translated in the Bible as well. We are to be low in spirit, meaning we are lower than Jesus. Jesus is higher than us.

Whether in life or in horsemanship, think of yourself as lower, do not be proud, and do not think you know everything. For those who do, deceive themselves. Every single moment is an opportunity to learn from Jesus, a horse, and others. Pray for discernment, direction, clarity, His wisdom, and knowledge.

Be wary of those folks who constantly refer to themselves, their own services, and have a "my way or the highway" attitude. You know those people, the ones who constantly look for a battle on the internet or in public. Steer clear of those folks who pick fights to voice their opinions with little respect for others. Be mindful and love those bullies from a distance. Those of Jesus, we are to be stewards with a purpose to walk with Him. The Lord shows us time and time again we are to act justly, love mercy, and walk humbly with Him.

"Walk humbly" is a description of the heart's attitude toward the Lord. As Christians, we should depend on the Lord rather than our own abilities (Micah 2:3). Instead of taking pride in what we bring to the Lord. We should humbly recognize that no amount of personal sacrifice can replace a heart committed to justice and love. The response of a godly heart is outward (do justice), inward (love mercy), and upward (walk humbly).

The message of Micah still applies today. Religious rituals, no matter how extravagant, can never compensate for lack of love (1 Corinthians 13:3). External compliance to rules is not as valuable in God's eyes as a humble heart that simply does what is right. The Lord's people should desire justice, mercy, and humility before the Lord. Whether in life or in horsemanship, what is your walk reflecting?

> He has showed you, O man, what is good. And what does the Lord require of you? To act justly and to love mercy and to walk humbly with your God.
>
> MICAH 6:8

Christian Understanding of Spirituality

In today's world, there are many ways to believe, influencing our children and adults. The devil so cleverly uses platforms such as the news, Facebook, TikTok, YouTube, Instagram, and music to sway our focus back to ourselves. Whether we realize it or not, we are influenced by all we take in. There are also many religions focused on self, created to justify worldly sin. We can be spiritual and still go to hell.

What do I mean? A spiritualist oftentimes is confused. They pick and choose what they believe in. Typically, they have a mindset of having zero consequences for their sinning. They have no one-set faith. They believe in everything and understand nothing. They have no standards. They may have a prideful outlook, or they may come off as humble and "low energy," going with the flow. In either instance, their god only exists in their mind. These delusional conclusions of being spiritual with their own made-up god are oftentimes worldly-based. I ran across a quote that said, "Change is where the woo meets the work." I've met plenty of "woo-woo" folks. They believe they can change a person's energy, adjust one's chi, call on the spirits, talk to dead loved ones, and offer healing from their own hands. You best pause, hard folks, and rethink all that. Where is there "energy" coming from? Our "woo" should be coming from only King Jesus. Without Holy Spirit woo, forget accomplishing any good works. Only Jesus can make the work *work*! It's never about ourselves. It's about pointing the lost back to Him.

This spiritualism is focused on self and false gods.

The exact opposite of having the Spirit of Jesus in one's life.

A Christian being directed by the One and Only Holy Spirit is not confused. A Christian follows the Lord's words, accepting our sinful nature, repents, and seeks the Lord to change and do better the next go-around. A Christian is not "woo-woo" self-motivated but Holy Spirit motivated. A Christian isn't looking out for oneself but is concerned for others. A Christian is not entitled to anything, unlike the mindset of the world.

So, what's my point? I'm glad you asked! Whether in life or in horsemanship, don't get distracted by the overwhelming selection of trainers. Pay attention to the details. Inspect their fruits. Where is there "woo" coming from? Is it coming from self? Or is it Holy Spirit driven? Are good vibes and energy being voiced? Or is Jesus being recognized and praised? Our focus should be on allowing Jesus to change us from the inside out, which, in turn, changes everything around us. If we want change in our horse, we must change first. We want change in folks around us. We must be the change first. Oftentimes, the Lord refers to Christians as being light. Don't take it at face value. Seriously, be a beacon of hope, love, and light. Reflect Jesus and take every opportunity to be spiritual in Christ Jesus, not self. For Jesus is the way, the truth, and life. When we are led by the Ultimate Trainer, those around us will see it.

We know that anyone born of God does not continue to sin; the one who was born of God keeps him safe, and the evil one cannot harm him. We know that we are children of God and that the whole world is under the control of the evil one. We know also that the Son of God has come and has given us understanding so that we may know Him who is true. And we are in Him who is true—even in His Son, Jesus Christ. He is a true God and eternal life.

Dear children, keep yourselves from idols.

1 JOHN 5:21

Grow in Grace and Knowledge

But grow in the grace and knowledge of our Lord and Savior Jesus Christ. To him be glory both now and forever! Amen.

2 PETER 3:18

To grow in grace does not mean to get more and more of God's grace necessarily. Grace, by definition, is unearned, unworked for. By His grace, God has forgiven our sins and given us full rights as His children in Christ. We really can't get more of that. But living under the grace of Jesus provides us a huge opportunity to grow spiritually stronger and deeper. That's how we grow in grace. We grow under the grace of God by growing our knowledge in Christ.

There are many available religions, just as there are many ways to teach horses. But there is only one truth. Not a religious practice, but it is, in fact, having a relationship with Jesus, just as there is only one truth available to teach horses, and that is natural. Real truth leads to growth in knowledge.

Don't get distracted by religious practices, don't get stuck by the use of step-by-step DVDs or thirty-day fixes.

Be willing to learn. Think simply, naturally, and embrace Jesus' character and wise words of guidance.

Whether in life or in horsemanship, if we take the time to develop the right relationship, we will acquire purpose, direction, and enlightenment on true leadership and followership roles.

I do not demand for everyone to believe the way I do. I believe in the healing power of prayer. I believe all I have is because of my Father, Jesus. My gift of teaching and training is a blessing from the Lord. I believe in every word of truth offered in the Bible. I ask that you be open to a perspective pointing to Jesus.

He is my provider, my healer, my strength, my courage, my wisdom, my peace, and my purpose.

All I can do is share with you truths that no doubt work and make sense. I do not sugarcoat information, just like horses.

You can take the information or not. I like to offer enlightenment, plant seeds, and pray that anyone who hears is open to wisdom.

As you go about your day today, be open to learning the truth. Voicing your opinion isn't necessary if it'll start an argument. For a fool doesn't bridle his tongue. Be mindful of your mouth. Instead of using it to tear down others and provide false information or gossip, use it to lift others with truth.

Questions are fantastic when they are asked from a place of humility, not out of spitefulness.

We don't get it right every time. I'm raising my hand!

Shake the dust off, get back in the saddle, ask the Lord for forgiveness, and be better the next go around.

> Pride only breeds quarrels, but wisdom is found in those who take advice.

PROVERBS 13:10

Incidents Are Not
the Same as Identity

Just because you acted like that or accepted that or participated in that or even have an ongoing struggle with that doesn't mean that it is who you are or who you will be tomorrow.

Who you are is not one and the same with what happened to you once, twice, or even fifty times. The person they saw then is not necessarily the person they will always be.

You are who your Father says you are. And you wear the regal robes that grace threw over your shoulders the moment you were adopted into the Body of Christ.

Whether horse or human, do not judge based on incidents in history. That is not you or the horse's identity. Your identity is in Christ. Stop living in the past. Stop beating yourself up. Stop clothing you and your horse with that nasty helmet of shame. Put on the helmet of salvation.

A reminder today—you are a new creation in Christ. Yes, we are not perfect. We all fall short of the glory. Take on each day as an opportunity to share the love of Christ, turn from your old self, and focus on all the promises that Jesus Christ shares with you through Scripture. For only true wisdom and knowledge come from the Lord if you seek after Him fully. Don't miss out on today's blessing by focusing on what happened yesterday.

> Take off the old self, which is being corrupted in accordance with the lusts of deceit and put on the new self, which in the likeness of God has been created in righteousness and holiness of the truth.

EPHESIANS 4:22-24

Stand on His Promises
Even in the Process

If you're believing for something today—finances, healing, deliverance, restoration of a relationship, there is a promise for you in the Bible—and one way or another, it is attached to an "if." Yet so many Christians stand on the promises of God, believing to receive, but don't fulfill the prerequisites. They like the idea of cashing in on all of God's promises, but they're less keen on mapping out the road to get there. Then, they're left wondering why it hasn't come to pass.

That's why so many people will declare, "I am the head and not the tail, above only and not beneath" (Deuteronomy 28:13), but don't forget about the rest of the verse: "If you pay attention to the commands of the Lord your God."

So, if you're standing on the promise of being the head and not the tail, above and not beneath in your job, your finances, your family, or any life situation—check the "if."

Are you paying attention to His commands?

Are you more focused on the reward of Christ versus being obedient to His Word?

Are you more focused on the end goal than learning from the journey?

Are you interested in horseback riding or all the things it takes to be a horseman?

Just as a mare's body takes time to form the sweetest bundles of joy. Each foal is meticulously formed in her belly, supplying all the nutrients needed for them to grow maturely. This should show you the importance of the process. If it's hurried along, complications can arise, but when you endure the journey, you will have a healthy reward.

To receive a full blessing from the Lord Jesus Christ, you must be willing to diligently seek after Him daily, not when you feel like it or when you're going through some heavy drama.

He is faithful to you ALL the time; you must be faithful to Him. You will only hear the voice of God if you have accepted Jesus as your Lord and Savior. With that, then the Holy Spirit will dwell in you. Without Jesus, you will only have a false representation of the One True Christ. The Lord isn't a vending machine of blessings. Have patience, keep the faith, stand strong on His Word, and be obedient to it ALL. Patiently endure the stumbling blocks and the process.

For the Lord turns those stumbling blocks into stepping stones to fulfill His prosperous dream for you.

With faith, you get started.
With patience, you finish the race.

Not only so, but we also rejoice in our sufferings, because we know that suffering produces perseverance; perseverance, character; and character, hope. And hope does not disappoint us, because God has poured out his love into our hearts by the Holy Spirit, whom he has given us.

ROMANS 5:3-5

Abednego,
Rescued From the Fire

BLM Freezebrand: #****4269
Rounded up from Triple B, Nevada

One of the most shared factual stories from the Bible is a narrative about three friends rescued from a fiery furnace (Daniel 3:1–30).

To summarize, King Nebuchadnezzar built an image of gold and commanded everyone to bow down to it. Whoever didn't worship this false idol was to be thrown into a fiery furnace. Some astrologers came to town and denounced these three friends who paid no attention to King Nebuchadnezzar's command. These friends went by the name of Shadrach, Meshach, and Abednego. The astrologers told the king they neither served his gods nor worshiped the gold image.

The king was enraged, and he summoned them.

When these men were brought before the king, he asked them if it was true that they did not serve his gods or worship the image of gold that he set up.

Shadrach, Meshach, and Abednego replied to the king that they didn't need to defend themselves before him in this matter. "If we are thrown into the blazing furnace, the God we serve is able to save us from it, and he will rescue us from your hand, O king. But even if he does not, we want you to know, O king, that we will not serve your gods or worship the image of gold you have set up" (Daniel 3:17–18).

The king was furious, and he ordered the furnace to be heated seven times hotter than usual and commanded the strongest soldiers in his army to tie up Shadrach, Meshach, and Abednego and throw them into the blazing furnace. The King's command was so urgent and the furnace so hot that the flames of the fire killed the soldiers who took up these three men. They were firmly tied and thrown into the blazing furnace.

King Nebuchadnezzar leaped to his feet in amazement and asked his advisors, "Weren't there three men that were tied up and thrown into the fire?" […] He said, "Look! I see four men walking around in the fire, unbound and unharmed, and the fourth looks like the son of gods."

Nebuchadnezzar then approached the opening of the blazing furnace and shouted, "Shadrach, Meshach, and Abednego, servants of the Most High God, come out! Come here!"

> So, Shadrach, Meshach, and Abednego came out of the fire, and royal advisors crowded around them. They saw that the fire had not harmed their bodies, nor was a hair on their head singed; their robes were not scorched, and there was no smell of fire on them.
>
> DANIEL 3:24-27

King Nebuchadnezzar was amazed as these three friends trusted in their God, Jesus, the One and Only True King, so much they were willing to give up their lives rather than serve and worship any false god other than their own. These three friends were a powerful example of the faith they had in Christ, which was a powerful example that King Nebuchadnezzar witnessed, which led him to change his heart.

As we are blessed to wake up each day, let us be an example to those to everyone, whether they know Christ or not. Display such profound faith that whatever hypothetical fiery furnace you're going through, know that the Lord Jesus is with you. He will pull you through it. You will not be harmed, and you won't be burned. Keep the faith. Be an example. Keep Christ first. Do not be thrown off track with false idols, for nothing will make you whole or complete you as Jesus will.

As you go about your work today, think before you speak. There is great power in words and names. This leads me to a profound revelation with one of the mustangs I've gentled. I'm honored to have named him Abednego. Day #5 was the day he was named after being picked up from holding. This completely wild horse has never been previously handled. Unfamiliar with the softness of human touch. We slowly but surely made strides in his gentling process. This mustang was a fiery, sweet gelding but very subtle with his warning signs of uneasiness. If he had been pushed too quickly, I'm confident he would have been aggressive. But those who are wise should know there isn't a need to push him to that level. A wise handler will quit before an explosion happens. Just as the Lord pushes us to grow, He never pushes us so hard to push us off the ledge. Approach your horse and day as such with gentleness, grace, love, and softness. Know that every day, when we are put to the test, Jesus is in the fire with us, and He will pull us out of it just in time.

Remember Whose You Are in Times of Discomfort

The Lord Jesus desires His children to give strength of testimony to each other. Whether in words or actions, all of it should be an example of Christ. Yes, we all fall short of the glory. Yes, we mess up. Yes, we are not perfect, and praise God for that! We should have a positive, faithful perspective to live our lives as Christ pours into us to build us up. Especially in difficult times. Those moments are true tests of faith in how we react, behave, and bounce back. Take every trial as an opportunity to trust Jesus Christ. Allow Him to mold you to be more like Him. Don't be discouraged! Remember, it's an absolute honor that our Father, Jesus, is willing to take the time to make us better if we allow Him to work. Just as we should take the time to pour into our works.

Whether you stubbed your toe, shut your finger in the car door, got a paper cut, got stepped on by a horse, got bucked off, got disqualified from the class, got cut off in traffic, got the pony finger, or the middle finger, was the moment handled in a way to glorify Christ?

If not, it's okay, but do better next time. Our shortcomings are available so we can learn from them. Don't be a repeat offender. Let the Lord change you. Every moment of discomfort is to push us closer to Christ. It's a reminder to trust in Christ in whatever we're doing and whatever we are faced with.

> Whatever you do, work at it with all your heart, as working for the Lord, not for men, since you know that you will receive an inheritance from the Lord as a reward. It is the Lord Christ you are serving.
>
> COLOSSIANS 3:23-24

Gifts Are Given to Be Shared

Leadership is about responsibility, not power. Whether with horses or in my faith, the Lord's character shines through.

My God has blessed me with an amazing talent that is an avenue to share my spiritual gifts. Gifts of the Lord's wisdom, understanding, knowledge, discernment, and, most of all, faith in Him.

Every single person on this earth has an amazing gift from the Lord. However, it's up to you on whether you use it (Romans 12:3–8). The beginning knowledge of what your purpose is comes first by accepting Jesus Christ as your Savior. For in Him, all things are possible. In Jesus, you can find your true motivation.

For the Lord does not bless His people with gifts to be only used at home in the presence of yourself (Luke 11:33; Proverbs 18:1–2).

In today's society, there is an overwhelming fog of laziness, pride, and "I can do it on my own" attitude. The YouTube gurus, self-help books, and worldly knowledge is unflattering and typically false, which fills people's heads up with arrogance (2 Timothy 3:2).

Without proper leadership, you will find yourself in a rut on the road to failure. You can't learn with a selfish, envious, judgmental attitude.

You can't learn without listening, and you can't grow without effective mentors. If you're questioning the actions of those you look up to, it's best to reevaluate their mentorship.

The most effective mentor to learn from is Jesus.

Every attribute of Christ I try my best to display in my horsemanship.

Our talk should match our walk.

I do not overpower. I lead by example with grace, love, humility, understanding, self-control, integrity, and praise (Galatians 5:22–23).

The character I show builds up the horse's faith in me, just as I have the upmost faith in my Lord and Savior.

For the only self-help book that guides you through the arena of life is the Bible. Do not be deceived by advice from other sources.

For those who slander, you are immature and lack knowledge. Those who are envious are weak. In such a time as that, pray for your brothers and sisters. Pray the Lord builds up their knowledge and opens their hearts and minds to His goodness.

When the Lord blesses you with a gift, you should have the desire to strengthen others with it (1 Peter 4:10–11).

Don't abuse it, or you'll lose it.

Gifts are given to be shared.

Misconception of Turning Thy Cheek

At first glance, we might think this verse teaches that no matter what someone does to us, we are to look the other way. We are not to take any actions against our aggressors. This could not be farther from the truth. This verse is not saying that we are to let people do whatever they want to us. Rather, it's saying God will handle it (Matthew 5:39 and Luke 6:29).

Looking deeper into Scripture, we find many examples of what Christians are to do when someone wrongs them. Looking back into the Old Testament, we see David sparing Saul's life again and again. First Samuel 26:9–11 tells us that David left the punishment of Saul to the Lord.

As Christians, we are going to face persecution. We may even get a slap in the face. We will be called self-righteous, arrogant, and be envied and hated without cause. But remember, so was Jesus. In these circumstances, we are never to get revenge. We are not appointed to punish the people who wrong us. We are to love them and let the Lord sort it out. God has the sole power to punish people who sin, not us.

As Christians, we must be careful that when we confront evil, we do not harbor a desire for personal vengeance. In Acts 23:1–3, Paul gives us a perfect example of how we should act when we are wronged. Paul is before the Sanhedrin exclaiming his duty to God when the high priest Ananias strikes him in the mouth. Paul's response was to inform Ananias that God would strike him. He then goes on to call out the fact that the Sanhedrin is judging him according to the law that they are also violating when they slap Paul. When we are wronged, we are to use the word of God to retaliate. In a gracious rebuke, we are to confront evil. Jesus did not say we were to stand aside and do nothing. He said that we were to confront the evils of the world by sharing the Gospel and praying for our enemies. We are to put on the armor of God and fight evil, not for personal gain but for the glory of God.

Whether in life or in horsemanship, you will be hated, just as the world first hated Jesus. If you belong to the world, it will love you as its own. The Lord wants so much more than what the world has to offer, just as a horse appreciates a right relationship versus a dictatorship. For every horse that I'm blessed to steward, I do my best to offer the right relationship. I do not alter my foundation based on a person's selfish desires or unrealistic expectations. I will not hurry a horse, and I will not go too slow where progress isn't made. I will not rush a young horse to be started under-saddle, and I will not cut corners when rehabbing or training an older horse.

It is disappointing to see progress made in a horse in

my care, then for it to leave, to be rushed into the hands of an ill-trained individual. Folks or "trainers" that ignore what the horse has to say are setting the horse up for failure. Being a cowboy or cowgirl is great, but it takes a true horseman or horsewoman to put a long-lasting foundation on any horse. Those who ignore horse behavior and/or herd dynamics lack depth in understanding why horses do the things they do. It's like knowing Jesus but ignoring scripture. You're missing out on all the goodness of daily tips, insights, and enlightenment to develop the right relationship. Folks who ignore this key component are putting their needs before the physical and mental readiness of the horse. The horse suffers because they want it to meet their expectations in an unrealistic timeframe. You should have more awareness of the details, and that's not available in the passing lane.

Jesus prepares a foundation for each one of us built on the right relationship. He doesn't rush us. He doesn't rough us up. He doesn't yank or jerk us around, demanding we carry more weight than we can handle.

Instead, the Lord gently guides us, carries our burdens, and offers an overflow of grace and love. Then He grows us in confidence and truth. The Lord works with us exactly where we are in our life, just as I work with the horse right in front of me. You can't make a confident, willing, trustworthy partner in thirty days, just as you can't master everything Jesus has to offer in thirty days. You must be willing to invest the appropriate amount of time to learn every day, not just when you feel like it. In both Christ and horsemanship, there's a big difference between a tolerant dictatorship and a willing partnership. I don't know about you, but I'm all in for a willing partnership.

A PRAYER FOR TODAY:

Lord, keep me focused on You. Remove the neigh-sayers from my life. Don't let me focus on the haters that try to discredit You or me. Don't let me get distracted by those who take credit for my works, which is a gift from You, and allow me to continue putting You first. Remove those from my life that have unrealistic expectations that will eventually bring danger upon themselves. Reveal that there is only death awaiting apart from You, Lord. Continue to put dedicated, committed, like-minded people in my life. Those that want to learn, love, and be ALL in. Lord, bless my enemies. May You tug at their hearts and speak to their souls. May they see there is more to life than personal gain, but there's so much more You have to offer with a Holy Spirit gain. Lord, I ask You to continue to give me the right words to speak, to be a light of You, and to confront evil without harboring vengeance. I ask repentance for anything that I have said, thought, or done that wasn't of You. Lord Jesus, keep making me more like You, and allow my works to continue to reflect Your love and light. In Jesus' name, amen.

Don't Drift Away
From Lord's Salvation

There are false teachers and false gospels in the world, meaning it's important for Christians to know the actual content of our faith so we won't be seduced by counterfeit versions. We must be able to understand our faith so we don't drift away from the truth.

Whether in life or in horsemanship, there are false teachers and false training methods. Some are focused on self-versus the relationship. Some are focused on the hand instead of the Handler. Some methods glorify liberty without foundational truth. A wild soul surely ends in despair without direction and boundaries to safety.

Don't fall victim to the trickery. The devil prowls around to kill, steal, and destroy. The devil throws us off track by presenting opportunities to glorify ourselves. Folks get hung up on how fast they can potty train a child or imprint on a foal. Folks who are focused on numbers instead of relationship haven't received the hope and promises of Jesus. Don't be fooled by fast-food methods and DIY programs. The Ultimate Trainer is available for a reason. Just because we can do many things doesn't mean we should. A jack of all trades is a master of none. It might be cheaper, but it'll cost us more in the end.

When our focus shifts to changing ourselves so we can affect those around us positively, that's the light of Jesus. Pay careful attention to the messages spoken. Eventually, there will no longer be an excuse as to why we didn't consider the Lord's salvation. It's never too late to put our hope and trust in Jesus. Lay down your confusion, anger, jealousy, pride, arrogance, slothfulness, tiredness, and every other burden imaginable, at the feet of Jesus. Let Him intervene and work on our behalf. For Christ is still in the miracle-working business, but we must allow Him to work. Stop running wild and find rest with the Ultimate Trainer. Allow the Lord to gentle you. Don't take all your burdens back. Bask in the Lord's confidence and truth, and trust in Him to move mightily.

We must pay more careful attention, therefore, to what we have heard so that we do not drift away. For if the message spoken by angels was binding when every violation and disobedience received are just punishment, how should we escape if we ignore such a great salvation? This salvation, which was first announced by the Lord, was confirmed to us by those who heard him. God also testified to it by signs, wonders and various miracles, and gifts of the Holy Spirit distributed according to His will (Hebrews 2:1–4).

Let Your "Yes" Be "Yes"
and Your "No" Be "No"

In a world that justifies lies and excuses, be different. It's not complicated, to be truthful. Self-justification isn't necessary. For godly justification doesn't come by giving a quick, drawn-out answer or proving one's innocence, but rather through repentance and remaining free from sin. Let the Lord guide your feet in this arena of life. No questions, just let Him lead you, just as my horses don't question my leadership.

Simply let your "yes" be "yes" and your "no" be "no." If you must swear beyond those simple truths, then they are nothing but empty words. Integrity is having an inner grit and grip with grace and humility. Display that in all that you do, including relationships. These simple truths can magnify any part of your life. But it starts with a change of heart that can reflect positive attributes that will last a lifetime. Whether you're swinging your feet into your vehicle or into the saddle, remember you are blessed! You are highly favored! Represent the One who gives you chances time after time, forgiving you of all your flaws, and honor the Lord to do your best every chance He gives you by being an example of His light and truth. Most of all, with integrity. Whether horse or human, we must be firm in our answers in love. We must have clear boundaries of what we are seeking, just as the Lord is clear and concise on what He wants from us. He doesn't justify His instructions. He just IS. He doesn't need to prove anything. He doesn't justify His "yes" and "no," for that alone is enough. He showed His love for each one of us on the cross. He reveals to us daily that we can turn to Him for His constant leadership and His never-ending love. He does not waiver. He doesn't straddle the fence. The Lord is never changing.

Just as I work with my horses and clients, I must remind myself to correct in firmness, in love, and mean what I say. Let my instruction be clear, with no justification, and be simple with a "yes" or "no." The closer we walk with the Lord, the more He will use us. The more committed I am to a horse, the stronger the communication becomes, and clarity is revealed on willing results. I allow them to find the answer and wait for that lick and chew of comprehension, a relaxed body, and softness in the face. The Lord wants to see the same relaxation in us.

He wants you to know He's got you through the pressure until the release is found, leading to that lick, chew, and state of relaxation.

Have confidence in Him, just as you ask your horse to have confidence in you with simple questions that can be answered with a "yes" or "no."

Simply let your "Yes" be "Yes," and your "No" be "No;" anything beyond this comes from the evil one.

MATTHEW 5:37

Lazarus,
Don't Doubt the
Lord's Power

BLM Freezebrand: #****7215
Rounded up from Antelope, Nevada

Time and time again, true narratives are shared throughout the Bible of the Lord's amazing power. However, there are many people who only believe in only realistic stories, change scripture to fit their lifestyle, or don't believe any of it at all. We silly humans sure have a knack for trying to figure out everything, have a reason or excuse for it all, and of course, justify our sins, choices, and lifestyle. If it doesn't line up with scripture, folks, it ain't the way to be livin'. An astounding thought, even if the Bible were false, what would be so bad about living a life with morals, standards, and an unseen hope? For those who know the Bible is truth, I have complete faith in that unseen hope. A never-ending infinite hope in Jesus. His grace, love, and life are something to always look forward to.

Let's look at a famous story Jesus shared in scripture about a man named Lazarus. There are two men named Lazarus in the Bible, but I'm specifically focused on Mary and Martha's brother, Lazarus. To sum up this passage in John chapter 11 (go read the whole thing for yourself), Lazarus had fallen sick. Word was sent to Jesus, and He waited two more days to head back to Judea, a place where people were waiting to kill Jesus. On Jesus' arrival in Judea, He found out that Lazarus had been in a tomb for four days. Martha went first to meet Jesus. Then Mary sought out Jesus. When Jesus saw Mary weeping for her brother, Lazarus, Jesus wept also. Jesus was deeply moved and went to Lazarus' tomb. Jesus called out Lazarus by name. The dead man came out, his hands and feet wrapped with strips of linen and a cloth around his face. Jesus said to them, "Take off the grave clothes and let him go" (John 11:44).

A few things the Lord revealed to me in this passage: Jesus is always near to call on, especially in sickness. Jesus loved Lazarus so much that He wept for him, just as He loves you and me. Jesus knowingly went into a dangerous place where He faced plots of His death to hear the cries of Lazarus' sisters. Jesus said time and time again, if you believe, you will see the glory of God. In this case, bringing Lazarus back from the dead. Jesus not only brought out Lazarus from the grave from physical death, but it was an example for those suffering spiritual death to have hope in Christ.

So, with all that being said, no matter what you face, pull yourself out of that pit, take off your grave clothes! Come alive in Jesus. Physical and spiritual illness will not lead to death but lead to glorifying the Lord. Lazarus' name means "God has helped." Just as God helped restore his life, I have the honor of restoring hope, purpose, and life in wildlies. Don't focus so much on death in this story but on the glory of who it honors. Whether in life or in horsemanship, Lazarus' story was and is used to share the glory of Christ. The Pharisees couldn't stop the truth of the power of Jesus, so don't let the enemy of the world stop the Lord's work in you! Keep believing, resurrect Jesus every day, be purposeful in your works, and let your Jesus' light shine!

I am blessed to share Jesus every day in my life and my works. Without further ado, the Lord revealed a name to me for yet another wild mustang. #7215 is no longer a number. It's now Lazarus.

The more I work with this quirky, playful, peaceful soul, the name of Lazarus really suits him. Lazarus reminds me daily to keep the grave clothes off. May the Lord give me wisdom to guide and help Him, just as He did Lazarus. Remember the power of Jesus is available to you when the Holy Spirit lives in you.

Dwell in the Land
and
Enjoy Safe Pasture

Trials and triumphs are always around the corner, which has brought about many tests of my faith. "How has the Lord worked in me to deal with these trying moments involving difficult people?" I'm happy you asked. Let me shed some light and share a testimony.

I've dealt with a handful of folks who have put their needs before their horses. They had the greatest intentions at the beginning, to send their horse to training. Then somewhere in all that, they decided to put their needs first. Their human needs for a fast-food training process came before the right relationship, built on faith and trust, to provide a successful future for their equine. Ever heard that saying: "The road to hell is paved with great intentions"? Well, it's true. People can have the greatest intentions but lack the commitment to follow through. You can't stay committed to anything by your own strength.

The light of the Lord will illuminate the plans of the undedicated. The Lord brings truth to the surface and exposes those who are arrogant, prideful, selfish, manipulative, broken, unconfident, overpowering, controlling, rude, and lost to the surface. The same applies to a horse. I see many times people lying to themselves in regard to what they know. They puff up a self-image of knowledge, which in turn damages a loving purposeful relationship with Christ, as well as damaging a secure right relationship with your horse.

In the end, these folks will learn the hard way, as they are too arrogant to receive help or advice. Pride goes before destruction, whether in life or in horsemanship. It can lead to a broken spirit or broken bones. So, don't wait until you're at your lowest point in life. But if you are to that point, it's never too late to accept Jesus in your heart. The Lord turns chaos into peace, despair into hope, pride into humility, rudeness into kindness, and gives you purpose in doing good in your life.

Whether in life or in horsemanship, motivators such as cookies provide false security in a human or horse. You can't bribe a horse to stay focused on you as all they see is the hand, not the Handler. False confidence masks the true nature of a horse or human from reacting or throwing a fit. It's a Band-Aid on a broken spirit. When brought to the surface in a horse or human, natural "tantrums" come out in a fight-or-flight manner. In those moments, how will you redirect, horse or human, to trust you? Will you entice them with cookies? Will you offer comfort in the right relationship? In order to have the right relationship, you must be focused on the Ultimate Trainer, who offers the truest training methods without temptation.

Some folks get so wrapped up in all the different

religions and training methods that they lose sight of truth and Natural Horsemanship. Don't be fooled by false prophets and false trainers. Cheaper isn't always better. Always put others and your horse before your desires. Live each day with hope instead of plotting evil or comparing yourself to others around you.

For I know the Lord has great plans for us, but we must be willing to allow Him into our hearts.

We shouldn't see other people as competition but as an opportunity to share the love and peace of Christ in our lives and works. You can't help those who don't want to be helped, but you have the choice to be the light of Jesus in tribulation. The Lord puts challenges in our lives to grow us in faith and character. It isn't easy. But it's worth it. Allow the Lord to work in you. It'll affect those around you, and pray for the lost no matter what.

Refrain from anger and turn from wrath; do not fret— it leads only to evil. For evil men will be cut off, but those who hope in the Lord will inherit the land. A little while and the wicked will be no more; though you look for them, they will not be found. But the meek will inherit the land and enjoy great peace.

Better the little that the righteous have than the wealth of many wicked; for the power of the wicked will be broken, but the Lord upholds the righteous. In this crazy world, don't fall victim to the pit of anxiety, stress, and misdirection. Allow yourself to be led by the Ultimate

Trainer, Jesus. He will make a way when there seems to be no way. He will bring you through it and give you victory leading to a safe pasture.

> Do not fret because of evil men or be envious of those who do wrong; for like the grass they will soon wither, like green plants they will soon die away. Trust in the Lord and do good; dwell in the land and enjoy safe pasture. Delight yourself in the Lord and he will give you the desires of your heart.
>
> PSALM 37:1-4

Some Simple Truths

If you can't trust the Lord to provide the small things, what makes you think He will provide the big things? The Lord isn't a genie in a bottle. You can't simply demand what you want, not put forth effort or works, and expect it to work out successfully.

The mentality that you can do this thing on your own with no guidance will certainly end in destruction.

To be successful and effective, you must trust Him with the small things first to build faithfulness. No faithfulness—no stability in your life.

These simple truths are not only ignored in life but even in horsemanship. I've seen many times folks will get a new, young horse and expect it to be capable of trail riding once a month with no issues without ever putting work in on the ground. I hear time and time again that arena work is boring, and they'd rather trail ride, go rope, or go show.

If you're not allowing your horse to be trusted with the small things on the ground in a round pen or in the arena, do you really think you have enough trust built in your horse to look to you for leadership trail riding in the Croatan Forest?

If you said no, good on you for being honest with yourself.

If you said yes, how does that ride look playing back in the theater of your mind?

Did your horse spook at something and go five miles sideways? Did you pull your pony out to ride him in the front yard after he's been sitting for a few months, and he went to buckin'? Did you decide to take up mounted shooting for a day, and he reared the first time you ever shot of him?

If you're still thinking yes and you got this thing on your own, you're fooling yourself. Granite horses are horses, they have a mind of their own, but when you have prepared your horse in the small things and built up the right relationship establishing trust with your mount, they'll look to you for direction, think more, and react less. However, that's another message, and let's get back to the main point being conveyed here: If you can't trust your horse with the small things, he won't be able to trust you either, as you have put no work or effort to build up a foundation for the right relationship.

But things are different if you build your horsemanship on a simple truth of trusting Him:

1. on the ground,
2. in the saddle,
3. riding in the round pen,
4. riding in the arena,
5. riding in big ole open spaces.

Whether in faith or in horsemanship, do not bypass the little things because you are so focused on the big things.

Horses and Christ do not have malicious intentions. You get out what you put in.

Preparation precedes success.

> Whoever can be trusted with very little can also be trusted with much, and whoever is dishonest with very little will also be dishonest with much.

LUKE 16:10

Faith is built in the process, not the end product.

My Teachings Are Not My Own

Jesus answered, "My teaching is not my own. If anyone chooses to do God's will, he will find out whether my teaching comes from God or whether I speak on my own. He who speaks on his own does so to gain honor for himself, *but* he who works for the honor of the one who sent him is a man of truth; there is nothing false about him."[1]

JOHN 7:16-18

My works are not my own, for I do my best to reflect Jesus in my life, as well as in my daily work.

My horsemanship is an ability given by God, a gift to reach folks using horses. The Lord prepared me as a little girl, instilling this desire and love that has forever captivated me. He gave me the words of the "breath of horse crazy" that was whispered into my soul from the beginning of time. The Lord continues to tug at my heart to change me to be used by Him. He has opened doors and opportunities for growth as I seek after Him and obey Him. For I didn't just wake up one day and think to myself, *Let me be a horse trainer. Let me stick a sign at the end of my drive and start a business. Let me blindly try to work with horses.* No. The LORD instilled this in me to use me to glorify HIM. He planned it meticulously from the

---

1 Emphasis added.

99

very beginning. He gave me knowledge first. He makes me capable of doing the works that are available successfully because He is ordering each step. He has given me the wisdom and knowledge to do my works to the best of my ability. He's given me the backbone to stand firm in Him when those try to come against me. His love, grace, and teachings reflect in my life and in my horsemanship.

In life and in horsemanship, there are many folks who claim to be trainers or mentors. But the Lord is the only worthy trainer to be under. He gives solid direction, but you must be willing to listen.

Don't be misled by uneducated people.

You can't be selfish, and you can't think you can do this on your own. When working with a horse, whether green or broke, it's best to work under someone educated first before trying to tackle things on your own. When you think you can do it all on your own, you are in for a rude awakening, making room for many errors. You open doors for mistakes and opportunities to get hurt or even killed.

Just as in life away from Christ, it's a harder journey doing things on your own. You leave room for many opportunities for the devil to swoop in and attack you, hurt you, or to even kill you, leading to eternal damnation. Allow the Lord to guide you and educate you. Let Him be the boss of your life. For He will put needed mentors in your life to help grow you.

Don't be consumed by selfish desires, money, or other things of the world, for those are distractions from your true purpose in life.

Surround yourself with educated folks, those who reflect what they teach. The Lord opens doors for His children. He will guide you with a righteous hand and pour out His blessings continuously.

Those who truly seek after Christ will focus on nurturing their relationship with Jesus. For the goodness of the Lord bares good fruit reflecting in your life. Good things bare good fruit, never becoming stale.

> [...] he who works for the honor of the one who sent him is a man of truth; there is nothing false about him.

> JOHN 7:18B

For the Spirit lives within the discipline of Christ, shining bright like a beacon of hope in an ever-changing, darkening world.

Reactions in Stressful Circumstances

This world today is crazier and filthier-minded than it used to be. Have you noticed a rise in death rates (not associated with COVID)? A rise in entitled-minded people, whether kids or adults? A rise in confusion, selfish attitudes, busybodies, a lack of respect for elders, the church, and most importantly, acknowledgment of sharing and knowing Jesus Christ. I've been told for years by my blessed grandpa, who's now with the Lord, we were living at the end of days, and I believe that now more than ever. If you're in the Lord's Word, it's evident scripture is revealing itself, and every day, it's coming closer to the Lord's return. If you aren't aware of His return or don't believe the Lord's return, seek out the Word and allow the Lord to educate you (Matthew chapters 24 to 25; Mark chapter 13; Luke 21:5–26; John 14:25–29; Revelation 16:15).

With that being said, people will face trials more, especially Christians.

I can only speak from what I have experienced. This new year has been hard for me, my family, and our ministry, but my faith has never wavered, and neither should yours.

I've been faced with the loss of loved ones, critters, difficult clients, growing amazing clients, roadblocks in the expansion of my ministry, unexpected and expected traveling, financial obstacles, and the list goes on and on. I have felt numb at times, struggling with the Lord's words to be still, wondering what I should do, what I shouldn't do, and a creep in of that sneaky devil trying to set fear and stress in, but God! He constantly reminds me to seek and stay in His will by praying and applying all of His Word to every minute of my life. I am not perfect. I would never claim that anyhow, as we all fall short of His glory. I do my best to be better than I was the previous day. In all the fiery trials, prayer has never left me. It shouldn't leave you either. The world will never encourage you, but Jesus' Word will. I look back to the experiences I have faced and our experiences now; I know Jesus will not lead me to failure. His Word says so. I know He will work it all out for the good of those who believe in Him. That, too, is another one of His promises. I'm joyful and hopeful of facing trials with Jesus on my side.

I've been guilty many times, finding comfort in this little phrase, "It could always be worse." But God!

What enlightenment the Lord has revealed, I shouldn't find comfort in this earthly saying. On many occasions, I've found comfort in Jesus Christ's Word. A reminder— my comfort should always come from scripture. It's His living Word and something that should never leave my heart. Even in the trials I am facing now. All those who are facing certain situations, as a Christian or not, it's my honor and duty to encourage you also with the word, not a shallow saying of, "it could be worse" or another type of worldly phrase. Phrases offer zero comfort in your trial. Oh! But the beautiful encouragement truths of the Bible (Basic Instructions Before Leaving Earth).

Just this week, I've been faced with many opportunities to share the love and encouragement of Christ. Instead of reacting selfishly, harboring discontent based on past encounters, or responding in anger, based on losing someone too soon, or ignoring certain circumstances because it made my flesh crawl with discomfort. I chose not to react on emotion or selfish desires. Instead, I acted on the wisdom of the Lord and His blessings to be refined by His godly character.

With every tragedy and triumph, there is a lesson. It's whether or not we are willing to be humble enough to be changed and learn from the situation versus being dragged down by the devil. Take the opportunity to not be offended but to be transformed with a Jesus perspective.

Long story short, this week in my travels, I'm guilty of saying after my truck was gifted with a Maryland souvenir, "It could have been a lot worse."

I find comfort in knowing the Lord had me covered under His wings. He protected me, my friend, my truck, and my horse trailer. I realize more every day, prayer is powerful. Just like my truck was armor around my friend and me, the Lord is my armor, suiting me up to take a stand against the devil scheme's wherever I go.

> Stand firm then, with the belt of truth buckled around your waist, with the breastplate of righteousness in place, and with your feet fitted with the readiness that comes from the gospel of peace. In addition to all this, take up the shield of Faith, with which you can extinguish all the flaming arrows of the evil one. Take the helmet of salvation and the sword of the spirit, which is the word of God. And pray in the spirit on all occasions with all kinds of prayers and requests. Be alert and always keep on praying for all the saints. Pray also for me, that whenever I open my mouth, words may be given me so that I will fearlessly make known the mystery of the gospel, for which I am an ambassador in chains. Pray that I may declare it fearlessly, as I should.

EPHESIANS 6:13-20

A Good Teacher

One of the characteristics of a good teacher is being a good learner and a good listener. Teachers should model for their students the value of learning. We can never learn all there is to know about teaching, nor will we ever have all the answers. If you don't know something, be honest about it and seek a valuable mentor for help.

For those who act like they have all the answers, humbly watch them, take mental notes, and ask questions. Teachers that don't try to learn themselves can unintentionally or intentionally teach you incorrectly. Inspect your teacher's morals as that will reflect what they are teaching. Make sure you understand what they're teaching. Do they know what they're sharing? Assuming a teacher role without the proper knowledge could lead to mishandling and misinterpretation. Some teachers are neither gifted nor morally qualified.

Whether in life or in horsemanship, a teacher should be held to higher standards. As a teacher, you should also have higher standards, doing everything you can to teach correctly and effectively. You shouldn't have the mentality of muddling your way through. You should want to offer a correct foundation for a horse and for yourself. "Fake it until you make it" is a shallow slogan of little effort.

Live freely and authentically in Christ, providing

yourself and your horse with a correct foundation with a right Teacher.

A good teacher should not have the desire for power and influence but should want to selflessly educate.

Good teachers are good learners. Those with the gift of teaching also love to continue learning. The best teaching arises from the heart of someone who is passionate about what God is teaching him or her (2 Timothy 2:15).

What kind of teacher do you have?

Not All Are
Qualified to Teach

Everywhere you look, someone is trying to sell you that they are qualified to teach you, your kiddos, or your horse. Now don't get me wrong, I'm not pointing out this simple fact to be ugly or start an argument, but to offer insight. Those who want to air opinions are fools. The wise keep their mouths shut to avoid arguments.

In today's self-motivated world, just for a minute, breathe and read with a perspective to learn. I want you to embrace a Jesus way of thinking. I want to offer enlightenment to encourage you and grow you. I want to offer you some Christ-like wisdom.

Whether in Christ or in horsemanship, it takes an individual willing to teach and preach, but it also means not everyone is called to do either of these things.

First, what is teaching? Whether it's in a school, at the barn, or leading by example in any other workplace on earth, the title of a teacher is a gift of the Holy Spirit (Romans 12:6–8; 1 Corinthians 12:28). Just as serving, encouraging, giving, and leading is mentioned. But let's stay on track here and get back to biblical truths of teaching.

The gift of teaching is given to edify the body, not self (1 Corinthians 12:7). When we teach, we shouldn't be teaching for recognition or because we want to be noticed. It's not about us but about a gift that the Lord has put inside of us to serve. The best way to know if our gift has been given to us is this—it's typically been affirmed in us by more than one person within the church. If not, then tread carefully.

A few mind-blowing points to consider discerning tricky from the truth:

*A teacher should be cultivated through spiritual growth. A person should be spiritually mature in their faith and what they're teaching. Whether in faith or in horsemanship, the fruits of the Holy Spirit should be reflected (Galatians chapter 5).

*A teacher must have proven to be reliable and experienced (2 Timothy 2:2).

*A teacher must be under a sound teacher (Luke 6:40).

Someone should not be teaching if they themselves do not sit under sound teaching. I would take it a step further; a teacher should also have a trainer, coach, and mentor. Being a teacher doesn't exempt us from being students. This exhibits a pattern of surrendering to authority, accountability, and correction.

*We are told not many should be teachers, and those who teach are judged with greater strictness (James 3:1–2), which makes it hard to believe that we can scroll through Instagram and find hundreds, if not thousands, of people claiming to be Bible teachers, ministry leaders, riding instructors, and horse trainers.

*A teacher must be above reproach, meaning people shouldn't be able to identify, by looking at your life, cause for sin or concern (Titus 2:7–8). This goes back to the fruits of the Holy Spirit.

Whether in life or in horsemanship, pay attention to the little things. How do the people and horses act around the assumed teacher? Is the environment peaceful or stressful? Is what's being taught being practiced? Are foundation, safety, and fun at the forefront of the mind of those claiming leadership roles? Are sound principles being offered and explained with the truth? Does their life, or yours, show good fruit?

Be careful, as cheaper isn't always better. Not all who teach are qualified. But know one thing, salvation in Jesus is a FREE gift that isn't cheap quality or unqualified. For He is the Ultimate Trainer and offers great wisdom and direction in whatever circumstance you face today. We are not perfect. We never will be. We all fall short of the glory. The Lord gives all of us a gift each day to be better and embrace more of His character and qualities. I challenge you to question those you choose to learn from. Ask questions and seek the truth.

For the utmost clarity and soundness of mind, I dare you to try Jesus and see what He provides.

Are You on the Right Path?

He (Jesus) calls His own sheep by name (He speaks to us personally) and leads them out (providing us with direction). When He has brought out all His own, He goes on ahead of them, and His sheep follow Him because they know His voice (they know His voice because they have spent time with Him). Refer to John 10:3–4.

He has gone before us and sees the dangers and trials we will face. He is telling us the way to go, the perspectives to keep, the things to avoid, and the things to hold fast to. Most of all, He is speaking to us because we are His own, and He wants a relationship with us. He loves us, adores us, treasures us, and has a good plan for us. He longs for us to know His voice and listen to His voice. The only way to know and trust God in this way is to spend time with Him.

> *When we invest in spending time alone with God, he will speak to us, and what we hear from Him in these quiet times will be echoed in other places. Listen for God's voice and then look for the message to be confirmed.*
>
> LYSA TERKEURST

Whether in life or in horsemanship, the Ultimate Trainer goes before us, just as I go before my horse. I take every measure to apply what the Lord teaches me, preparing a way to build a correct foundation, a common language without words, and keeping His character at the forefront of my mind. The Lord what's us to listen to Him, not to exert a sense of authority in a person's life or to simply boss us around, but the Ultimate Trainer is seeking an ear that's willing to hear. He wants us to listen because He loves us, adores us, treasures us, and wants only the best for us.

When training a horse, I put in limitations and a clear understanding of building a correct foundation on willing obedience. Then this will translate past tolerance because trust and love have been established in the right relationship in my leadership role. All because I love every mount I work with, I adore them, I treasure them, and I want the best for them, but I can never love them as much as the Lord loves me. The Lord also loves you more than you could ever imagine, but you must be willing to heed His direction and listen to His Word to stay on the right path.

Radically Blessed

The other day, I was driving down a busy road when I came upon a traffic light that was both green and red at the same time. I slowed down, unsure what I should do, as did other cars coming from all directions. It was a confusing and dangerous situation. Some people stopped. Others ran through the light, and still others pulled off to the side of the intersection.

I finally made it through the intersection and thought about what had just happened. It was if God were showing me a visual picture of what it's like when a person is indecisive in her obedience to him. We can't seek to follow God wholeheartedly if part of our heart is being pulled in a different direction. We can't pursue the radically obedient life and still continue to flirt with disobedience in certain areas of our life. We can't be both red and green toward God at the same time.

It gets us nowhere.
It's confusing.
It's dangerous.

LYSA TERKEURST

Whether in life or horsemanship, you have to be decisive. You have to be 110 percent committed to sticking with your choice and seeing it through. In horsemanship, when I'm gentling a mustang, I make sure I take every moment to be clear about what I'm seeking. If I'm seeking out a first touch or the triumphant moment of getting that tag off, I go about it in a manner of patience and kindness. I am willing to take direction from the Lord, and I'm considerate to what my horse is saying to me. I am wholeheartedly seeking that horse's focus. When I lose it, I redirect their feet and reward the slightest try.

When a person is only half-focused or tries every method under the sun only once, it will get you nowhere.

It's confusing.

It's dangerous.

You will not see results if you are being indecisive in how you're building your conversation and relationship with your horse. When you are not making progress, when you are feeling discouraged, do a self-check. In building the right relationship with Christ and your horse, are you displaying red and green tendencies at the same time? Are you being lured away by false methods? Are you too focused on the end goal versus seeing the magic in the purpose of the process?

There is power in the gentling process. You are preparing the horse's heart to better receive you, just as the Lord prepares our hearts in the waiting process to better receive His blessings in our lives. Do not be discouraged. Do not lose faith and hope in the One and Only King

Jesus, for He knows what we need more than we think we do. Jesus is the way, the truth, and the life. He is the Constant, He gives purpose, and He is clarity. We must keep two eyes focused on Him, and everything else will fall into place.

> You will seek me and find me when you seek me with all your heart.

> JEREMIAH 29:13

Knowledge Puffs Up,
But Love Edifies

A different perspective: Whether in life or in horsemanship, educating should be founded on love, not what we know. Knowledge puffs up, it swells egos, but love edifies, enlightens, and improves. Have you ever listened to pastors preach fire and brimstone, focusing on "you're going to hell if you don't accept Jesus"? Now all that is true; however, the message isn't received well as it isn't delivered in love. It feels more like condemnation than Holy Spirit conviction.

Have you seen horse trainers work with horses in a forceful manner and blindly go through the motions? They have all the knowledge in the world but no love or awareness to create a partnership. These trainers produce robots built on arrogance. There's a lack of choice in establishing boundaries.

Whether in life or in horsemanship, love should be the forerunner of the request. Grace should be next. Then wisdom added to seek guidance from Christ. This allows us humans to pour love into building up friends, family, acquaintances, and horses. We must be careful with our flesh consciousness so it doesn't become a stumbling block to ourselves and others.

I am blessed with my husband, my family, my friends, and my mentors, who pour into me knowledge built on love. I am blessed with the Holy Spirit, providing conviction and understanding, shaping me to be more like Him. I am blessed for my pastor, his wife, and our church that shares the message truthfully in love. I am blessed for my enemies, the ones that give me fake smiles and looks of stone. It brings me awareness to stay humble, continue every step in love, and keep shining my Jesus light bright. For my enemies are on a journey of change.

May the Lord enlighten you. May Jesus change your course to embrace selflessness. May you find mentors who pour into you with loving knowledge instead of arrogance. For our battles are not with other people but with darkness in the world. Always love the person and hate the sin.

For you will get much further in any goal when the Lord is guiding you. For He is the Ultimate Trainer.

> For our struggle is not against flesh and blood, but against the rulers, against the authorities, against the powers of this dark world and against the spiritual forces of evil in the heavenly realms.

EPHESIANS 6:12

Dreams Are
Purposeful Visions

A dream comes through much activity, and a fool's voice is known by his many words.

ECCLESIASTES 5:3

Dreams don't come true when more time is spent talking about them then praying and working toward achieving them.

THE POWER OF A PRAYING WIFE, STORMIE OMARTIAN

This.

Reading this scripture and passage brought a message to mind from the Lord to share.

I can only speak about what the Lord has brought me through, as well as how He continues to work.

His vision is my dream. My life had no purpose until I woke up and finally let Jesus in.

My dream as a little girl was to do anything with horses. Never in my life did I think it would be like what it is today. The Lord has allowed it to be far greater than I could ever imagine!

The Lord has made our equine business a unique place that stands out in our area, as well as in the industry. A place that stands the test of time in a community that's always changing. We take into consideration what our clients' wants are but never base our choices on wants. We ultimately want to give what they need. Because the need for truth, respect, grace, understanding, and words backed up by action should be offered far beyond wants.

My prayer is as our ministry continues to grow. May you see what the Lord has done and what He can do, not us. He moves mountains and makes a way if your will is His will. One of many favorite things my pastor (among many other things) says to newfound believers is to stay plugged into a truth-preaching church. I feel this is so relatable to everything we expose ourselves to daily.

Choose places and people that speak truth and life, and offer goodness for your soul. So, why not apply that to where you ride horses, motorcycles, play ball, shop, or eat? Feed your soul with good things.

Be Spooky, Be Brave,
Be Bold in Christ

Quiet people make spooky horses, and spooky people make quiet horses.

WYLENE WILSON

Don't tiptoe around your horse. Horses are quite predictable when we take the proper approach to prepare them. People, on the other hand, can be very unpredictable. When we try to be as smooth as silk or quiet as possible around a green horse, we're making an unconfident, spooky horse. The Lord doesn't tiptoe around us. He wants to form us, grow us in trials, and expose us to the fire so we can be changed. Do the same to your horse! Now calm down, I don't mean to literally expose your horse to fire, but I do mean expose them to "scary," unpredictable circumstances.

Accidentally drop a brush while grooming. Randomly gasp or scream as if a spider fell on your face. Grab your leg as if it were cramping because you forgot to stretch beforehand. Put on that rain slicker or coat, zip it up, make a song with Velcro, and sing while riding. Have a dance party around your horse. Wiggle the saddle, use that training flag, and play lots of friendly games with that carrot stick and string. Have fun! Be loud, don't be afraid, be you, embrace His Spirit within you, be courageous, and offer confidence and leadership to your horse, just as Jesus does for you. For the Lord builds our confidence by exposing us to spooky people and spooky circumstances. Offer the same for your beloved mount.

> For the Spirit God gave us does not make us timid,
> but gives us power, love and self-discipline.

2 TIMOTHY 1:7

Cheaper Isn't
Always Better

Just because you can afford the cheap cost of adopting a wild burro or mustang doesn't mean you have any business owning one. Be aware of the time and experience it takes in gentling and training an equine in general.

Be sure to have someone experienced and qualified to work with you if you're uneducated. Unfortunately, I've seen cases where horses come to me and must be restarted or retrained because of being handled improperly. There is no success in forcing an animal to do what you want.

Education is key!

The mindset to be willing to learn will get you way further than acting like you can do it on your own.

*The more you talk,
the less you know.*

You learn by listening.

Horses are dangerous if you are clueless, and mustangs are just as dangerous. They can bite, rear, kick, strike, drag you, and even run you over. So, be mindful, be safe, and don't be complacent.

Do your research when looking for mentors, as there are tons of people out there who claim to be amazing, qualified trainers with tons of degrees who aren't what they're advertising.

Paper means nothing to a horse.

Experience is everything and especially from who and how they've learned it!

I am a professional. I don't know everything, nor do I ever claim that.

I am humble.

I am confident.

I am always willing to learn.

I am a student.

I am a mentor.

I have professional mentors to further my ability because I always want to be growing in my field. My reputation speaks for itself, as does my character and my personal horses and horses I've trained.

In your journey of horsemanship, don't dismiss those who want to help you be better. It's a blessing to have elite riders who want to see you shine! I would know. I have some AMAZING professional trainers in my life who push me. I can't ever say thank you enough to y'all. Words can't express how appreciative I am to have y'all in my life.

Don't be prideful. Don't be boastful. Don't be demeaning to others. Be a light to others around you. Always take the time to lift others up.

Most of all, be happy for others and be thankful!

What you have is all blessings from the Lord that can be taken away in a nanosecond.

Our God gives us everything we need and makes us everything we're to be.

> Grace and peace to you from God the Father and the Lord Jesus Christ. We ought always to thank you God for you, brothers, and rightly so, because your faith is growing more and more, and the love every one of you has for each other is increasing.
>
> 2 THESSALONIANS 1:2-3

His Star of Bethlehem

Freezebrand: #****6785
Rounded up after Nevada, born in holding

A rescue mission took place in November of 2021 to pick up a BLM filly. The sweet filly settled in nicely at the farm. Due to no fault of her own, the owner simply wasn't in a good place to care for her. She had been shifted around, not fed consistently, and was labeled as a burden and a jerk.

She is far from these things. She may be head shy, but she is the sweetest baby. Consistently, she approaches me when entering her corral. This filly has surprised me with her gentleness and the want to be groomed and loved on.

As I had the chance to spend some time with her, I believe in the power of names. For those who know the power in the name of Jesus, even demons tremble at His name (James 2:19).

I feel we should recognize the power in names, even if it's a pet.

Her name is "His Star of Bethlehem." Around the barn, she will be called Bithia.

The Hebrew meaning of Bithia is "the daughter of Yahweh," for we all belong to the Lord Jesus, including the beautiful creatures He has made on this earth, giving us the opportunity to have dominion and stewardship over. Before Jesus' birth, "His Star of Bethlehem" was shown to the wise men. Jesus was born to save all people from their sins. His star was made visible to those wise enough to seek His presence. His star is more than just a celestial body. His star is the Shekinah glory, the dwelling of God, His Holy Spirit, that offers guidance, peace, relief, and a future of blessings.

May Bithia, "His Star of Bethlehem," be a reminder today that you are not a burden. Your fear, your anxieties, and your pain are never too much for the Lord. Lay down all the labels at His feet.

Jesus always provides the way. He is the light, He is the Shepherd of all, and He is willing to carry our burdens.

> Come to me, all you who are weary and burdened, and I will give you rest. Take my yoke upon you and learn from me, for I am gentle and humble in heart, and you will find rest for your souls. For my yoke is easy and my burden is light.
>
> MATTHEW 11:28-30

Scars of Sustaining Grace

BLM Freezebrand: #****3456
Rounded up from North Stillwater, Nevada

In my line of work, my husband and I often get calls to take in rescues. Update on the two rescues Josh and I took in from Richlands. The more we work with Jet and Storm, the more we are humbled. I want to take a minute to focus on Storm a bit. She's a BLM (Bureau of Land Management) mustang. She was thought to be five. However, it's been confirmed she's sixteen years old, born in 2002. I am trying to figure out a little bit more about her, but I won't be focusing much on her past, just as Lord doesn't focus on mine. Now that Storm is in our care, she's starting fresh. She's been baptized and washed clean. She has been brought out of her old life into a new one. I'll start to instill in her trust and confidence that I can be a worthy leader. I'll extend much-needed grace to her, just as she has to me.

Grace saves us through Jesus Christ. It sustains us through all trials. Trials make us stronger and more resilient, just as this mustang has resilience in moving forward from all she has endured. So, as I look at her old name Storm, she's endured many storms, she's moved around like unpredictable weather, and then the Lord led her down our path. As she's been washed and cleaned from her rainy and cloudy days, she's now starting fresh, covered in the Lord's grace.

Grace doesn't prevent pain, but it orders and arranges every step. The scares you live with are memorials of sustaining grace. As far as Storm goes, she will now be known as Grace. A much more fitting name for her, as she demonstrates such kindness in every expression. She demonstrates a never-failing grace to me, just as my Father does.

> But he gives more grace. Therefore it says, "God opposes the proud, but gives grace to the humble."
>
> JAMES 4:6

A Better Way

In this life, there are always better ways to do things. To achieve growth, whether with your horse or in life, your mindset must change. Do not focus on the old things, how you were mistreated at the grocery store, that guy who cut you off in traffic, the horse who gave you "the evil eye," and so on. People may have malicious intentions, but a lot of the time, we are just too selfish to notice the oopsie we just did, too easily offended, and sometimes too stubborn to care.

A beautiful thing about horses and Jesus, they do not think like us silly humans. They want to reveal our true purpose and help build us up to greatness. It's just whether or not we are open to the change.

So, wake up, oh, sleeper! Lay down yourself and pick up your cross daily. Meaning, focus on Jesus instead. Then the by-product will be self-help.

If only more folks had the attitude of being a student than the head honcho trainer. We would open ourselves up to so much more wisdom and, dare I say, kindness. Today, I challenge you with a different mindset. A positive outlook and the thought of, *What is Jesus trying to teach me?* I have this same outlook with every horse I work with. I do not have the selfish mentality of, "I'm going to teach this horse something," but rather, "What will I learn today?"

Leave your head trash and burdens at the arena gate.

Be willing. Be teachable. Be coachable. Be lovable. Be okay with being pushed out of your comfort zone.

Far more can be accomplished with a relationship of consideration of the other horse or human versus a complicated complainer and a demanding dictatorship.

For the Lord gives the opportunity for a better way of life under His coaching. For He is the way, the truth, and the life. Jesus is a beautiful light in this crazy, oppressed world.

> Do not offer the parts of your body to sin, as instruments of wickedness, but rather offer yourselves to God, as those who have been brought from death to life; and offer the parts of your body to him as instruments of righteousness. For sin shall not be your master, because you are not under law, but under grace.
>
> ROMANS 6:13-14

Seek *Him*, Not What

Smell is the horse's primary means of recognition. Giving the horse an opportunity to smell unfamiliar objects can help to reduce sympathetic arousal. Far too often, humans do not give the horse enough time to perceive objects by smell and to become comfortable with an unknown odor.

Horses will often loudly produce forced exhalations which sound like a snorting when unsure or sympathetically aroused. They do this in order to clear the nasal passage and to ready the nasal cavity to take a rich sample of the airborne molecules. Smells are turned into neural impulses by chemical receptors located in the nasal tissue.

> *Horses also have what is called a vomeronasal organ which features long tubes that line the mucous membranes. The tubular vomeronasal organs work by expanding and contracting like a pump when stimulated by certain odors such as pheromones and urine, driving their contents to their destination. In fact, the horse will often produce a flehmen response—an upward curling of the upper lip that helps to trap pheromones in the vomeronasal organ for further and closer analysis.*
>
> EVIDENCE-BASED HORSEMANSHIP,
> DR. STEPHEN BLACK AND MARTIN BLACK

What does all that fancy scientific stuff mean? In simple terms, there is a distinct difference in allowing your horse to smell something and feel something with its whiskers. Horses can already smell a person or item from several feet away. Knowledge is power. If you allow yourself to be a student of the horse and learn how a horse naturally functions, thinks, processes, and perceives requests, you will develop a strong foundation built on the right relationship. Horses are not dogs. Dogs are not horses. Horses think as prey. Where most other animals think as predators, just as people do.

The better you understand the horse, the better your training methods can be. Build a relationship with your horse, not a dictatorship. Allow the horse to seek who (you), not what.

Whether in life or in horsemanship, the Lord gives each one of us plenty of opportunities to smell the roses, pet the alligator, touch the stove, and become familiar with unknown objects, smells, and circumstances throughout the arena of life. Every opportunity is a pathway giving us an opportunity to either seek Him or seek what. Some of us choose to follow the Ultimate Trainer, while some get distracted by shiny and sparkling things.

Even when we fall short and choose the treats over the Trainer, He is still waiting for us to get back on the right path leading to Him. For the Trainer provides comfort, confidence, fulfillment, and stability far more than what can.

The Lord is always there waiting to pick us up, redirect our feet, and set our minds right.

We should demonstrate this same faithfulness, redirection, and grace to our horses as the Lord offers it to us. Jesus and horses never have malicious intentions. They put out what you put in. So don't give up when it gets tough. The Lord has never left you stranded.

> Jesus is always by your side, waiting to redirect your steps. For He is the way, the truth, and the life. No gimmicks, no tricks, no treats, just truth built on love, peace, joy, patience, goodness, kindness, gentleness, faithfulness, and self-control.
>
> GALATIANS 5:22-23

Faith in His Understanding

I do my best to demonstrate the characteristics of Christ in my horsemanship by building on the right relationship.

I do my best to show I am sincere, leading with love, and I am invested in every moment. I demonstrate grace to each horse I work with just as Jesus shows me daily grace. I constantly seek the right relationship built on the faith of a firm foundation. I do not hold grudges or try to breeze in once in a blue moon demanding attention.

I am constant, just as He is constant in my life.

I dedicate myself daily to seeking after right relationship to maintain and grow it.

Maturity in a relationship with Christ gives us the knowledge to learn to be respectable and hospitable. The Lord gives us the tools to teach His ways if we allow Him to use us. Every mistake I make, the Lord graciously grows me and corrects me.

The Lord has a plan for us. He is constantly seeking after us to love us and change us for the better. Stop running.

When we lack a relationship with Christ, we look like nuts, running around aimlessly. We find no satisfaction in chasing after worldly things. Comparable to those who lack a relationship with their beloved equines. Picture someone running around in circles in a horse pasture, cracking a whip to get their horse's attention. The more pressure they seem to put on that horse, the more they ignore the human. If the human had a right relationship with that horse, meaning a strong foundation built on consistency of faith and trust, the horse would seek after that human. He would have the want to join up with the person instead of running to his herd mates.

Let the Lord tame your inner rogue mustang and allow His guidance to put us on a straight purposeful path.

The Lord continues to seek after us just as He watches over every mustang lost in the desert. He wants nothing more from us to put our attention on Him. He chases after us like a nut running after their horse in a pasture. He loves each and every one of us like crazy.

Allow the Lord to find you and change you before the cracking of the whip sounds. All He wants is for you to join up with Him. Seek after Him wholeheartedly and allow Him to work through you. Do not be led astray by rogue spirits. For the Lord gives us such grace, mercy, and peace. He is the way, the truth, and the light. He is the rock of a successful relationship. We shouldn't have faith built on our own understanding or our own strength—for it's unsure and has a consistent failing foundation.

A right relationship is what should be sought after with Christ Jesus. The goal of this command is love, which comes from a pure heart and a good conscious and a sincere faith.

1 TIMOTHY 1:5

We're Not Wise

Brothers, think of what you were when you were called. Not many of you were wise by human standards; not many were influential; not many were of noble birth. But God chose the foolish things of the world to shame the wise; God chose the weak things of the world to shame the strong. He chose the lowly things of this world and the despised things— and the things that are not—to nullify the things that are so that no one may boast before him. It is because of him that you are in Christ Jesus, who has become for us wisdom from God—that is, our righteousness, holiness, and redemption. Therefore, as it is written: "Let him who boast, boast in the Lord."

1 CORINTHIANS 1:26-31

The Lord breathes in our dreams to glorify His name. It is up to us to listen. The Lord picks the weak, and He makes us strong. He chooses the lowly things and despised things and gives them meaning.

He chose you, just as He chose me to work for Him and to glorify His name.

Even though I am despised by others, my name doesn't leave the lips of those who wish failure upon me, and I am envied. I will not perish. I will not fail.

My work as a business owner and a horse trainer is non like others around. I have principles not only in my flesh but in my work. What makes me so different?

I know I am a sinner saved by the Lord's grace. I instill the Lord's principles in my training, such as trust, confidence, and grace, and show those around me that they are worthy. Just as the Lord shows me daily. I have the Lord's wisdom, who continues to show me what to do and how to live. I have the Lord's strength in me to be courageous to overcome and not fear any situation I'm put in.

Whether it's in a therapy session with a combative client or a training session with a combative horse, the Lord gives me the skills to discern the next move.

What makes me different as a horse trainer compared to others? Or a person?

Questions I have asked myself a million times. Oh, what a revelation! I am different as a horse trainer and a person because I'm a woman of God. I acknowledge I need Jesus Christ every minute of every day. I parallel my everyday life to my everyday work with horses. I accepted Jesus Christ many years ago to be the foundation of my life, to be my worthy trainer, and to lead me. He has filled the emptiest dark holes in my life. He has made me whole and filled me with His light and love. As I allow Him each day to continue to make me better. He reveals something new to me each time I read His Word or speak to Him in prayer. He has given me the knowledge, understanding, and purpose to be a whisperer of horses. He gives me the ability to communicate beyond words, just as He does with the Holy Spirit in us.

Like a wild mustang, that are despised things. Mustangs are considered nuisances, destroyers of crops, and a waste to protect. I, too, once felt like that. I was a rogue soul before I allowed the ultimate Trainer in my life to gently me. The knowledge of the world is foolish, but the power of Christ trumps the world.

I put aside my feelings and show compassion and pray for those around me. I don't let any of the negativity bother me because I am a daughter of a King, a child of the Highest, and my dreams are of the Lord. I boast not of myself, but I boast in the Lord. I continue to strive to grow in my faith and in my purpose.

Overlook those who hate you and speak lowly of you, for they do not know you. Hold your head up high and continue to work for the Lord. Let His light shine through you. Make the demons in your way tremble.

Strive to be better than you were yesterday.

Rest in the Lord's Truth
When Facing Sorrow

You will be missed, little Bithia. I am blessed with the life the Lord has given me this far. I'm blessed with an amazing husband, a fabulous equine vet, and wonderful clients, who are mostly my friends, and I get to live the ultimate dream as a horse trainer and instructor. The Lord has blessed me with a powerful gift to be gentle, train, and learn from a wonderful animal, such as the horse. With all these wonderful moments, sometimes sorrow is intertwined. It's always a hard choice to let go of something you grow close to, whether it's a person, a pup, or a horse. Over the last few years, it's been a privilege to be an approved trainer through the Mustang Heritage Foundation (MHF) and the Bureau of Land Management (BLM). It's an honor to be called by the organization without a thought to go pick up mustangs from unfortunate situations.

November 4, 2021, was one of these special cases where BLM asked me to go pick up a mustang filly to foster. A four-hour commute there and back, and we brought her safely back to Trail of Faith Farms (TOFF).

After proper care of working, farrier, and vetting, we found out this sweet girl had a broken lower leg that healed incorrectly, causing arthritic discomfort and would eventually cripple her. Being a "foster mom," I made one of the hardest decisions but the best choice with little Bithia's quality of life in mind. This decision was not made quickly. It consisted of many prayers, chats with my sweet and supportive hubby, valuable conversations with my vet, and consultation with the NC BLM rep. Little Bithia has grown so much here in TOFF's care. She has been loved by many special people. Absolutely spoiled with excellent care, handling, training, long hand walks down the road, ample amounts of hand grazing, plenty of feed, snacks, hay, and countless carrots. Little Bithia will always hold a special place in my heart. I believe I can say that for many others as well.

My earthly father passed away in 2010. Before he passed away, he sent me a box of goodies, horse magazines, family trinkets, shirts, and my favorite item, a burgundy foal halter. At the time, I had two adult horses and absolutely no need for a foal halter, but I kept it because my dad had sent it. Fast forward to now, it's unreal to see how the Lord orchestrates every moment in our lives. To include this silly foal halter I thought I'd never use, but I did... It fit sweet Bithia perfectly. Every moment was already planned out by my heavenly Father. What a blessing! And to know the Lord has a special purpose for horses, too, as He's coming back on a white horse with His armies following, I find comfort in knowing that Bithia will be a part of His army. She was a fighter until the very end. She was kind, courageous, confident, gracious, sassy, sweet, and a blessing to steward. I know I'll see you again someday.

Remember that God is with you. Jesus sits with you in your sorrow—even when all you can do is sit in silence. If you're facing the grief of saying goodbye, take a few moments to rest in the truth of God's Word:

> Everything on earth has its own time and its own season. There is a time for birth and death, ...for crying and laughing, weeping and dancing, ... embracing and parting.
>
> ECCLESIASTES 3:1-2, 4-5

Something Will Go Right

It may be difficult to maintain the right attitude with technology on the fritz, a house that hasn't been cleaned in weeks, facing sickness, a life-changing deal falls through, challenges arise at work, on the road, or in the arena, it's important to look to God for that change in perspective. We can trust that during all the things that seem to go wrong, something will go right.

In the struggle, we must keep our eyes looking up. Ask the Lord to give you His perspective to see past the struggles when things aren't going right. Ask Him to see the circumstances through His eyes instead of our own. Allow the Lord to speak His strength, boldness, and peace, for He has far greater plans for us according to His purpose. Don't give up. Don't give in. Don't allow the circumstance to steal our praises to the Almighty Father.

Whether in life or in horsemanship, there is a test to build our testimonies to glorify the Lord.

Keep holding on until the Lord makes all things right.

> Consider it pure joy, my brothers and sisters, whenever you face trials of many kinds, because you know that the testing of your faith produces perseverance.
>
> JAMES 1:2-3

Rejoice always, pray continually, give thanks in all circumstances; for this is God's will for you in Christ Jesus.

1 THESSALONIANS 5:16-18

Who's Leading Who

Oftentimes when I'm starting horses, I'll pony the horse in training off the horse I'm riding. Hence the term "ponying." This can be a great tool when used properly. Just like everything else available to learn these days, information can be used incorrectly or interpreted wrong without having a proper foundation. I've seen some trainers who use this ponying technique when they lack knowledge and confidence in starting horses. These trainers end up disregarding building the right foundation. Instead of teaching the horse to seek the trainer's leadership, the horse seeks guidance from the horse it's being ponied off of.

To successfully pony any horse in training, a proper foundation must be built first between you and the horse on the ground.

Take the time it takes, and it'll take less time.

Then once the horse knows it can come to you for confidence, comfort, safety, play, and guidance, you can incorporate such exercises as ponying.

So, what's my point of all this?

Well, I'm glad you asked. Whether in life or in horsemanship, a proper foundation with the Ultimate Trainer must be in place before other horses (or people) are added to the mix. The Ultimate Trainer is your main source of strength, direction, guidance, confidence, and peace. Where family, friends, the church, your pastor, mentors, and other horses are resources.

Make sure you're following the Source, not the resource.

Resources are available to make an already strong foundation stronger.

A poorly educated person and horse will ultimately come unhinged and stray from the right path, following the resource instead of the Ultimate Trainer in you.

> Yet for us there is but only one God, the Father, who is the source of all things....
>
> 1 CORINTHIANS 8:6A

> Do not conform any longer to the pattern of this world but be transformed by the renewing of your mind. Then you will be able to test and approve what God's will is—his good, pleasing and perfect will.
>
> ROMANS 12:2

Rich Without Understanding

When we trust in wealth, we are sealing our fate in the lake of fire. When we trust in Jesus, we will have a purposeful lead life worth living for. A life of abundance, overflow, and peace that surpasses all understanding, wisdom, and more. Don't try to keep up with the Joneses. The Lord has us all on specific paths for a reason. Stay focused on Him and watch Him bless you, not just with money and things, but things of more value, such as His clarity and character. The Lord will carry you and guide you, but you must be willing to be caught, stand at the tie post patiently, and let the Ultimate Trainer lead you.

Do not be overawed when a man grows rich when the splendor of his house increases; for he will take nothing with him when he dies, his splendor will not descend with him.

Though while he lived, he counted himself blessed— and men praise you when you prosper—he will join the generations of his fathers who will never see the light of life.

> A man who has riches without understanding is like the beast the perish.
>
> PSALM 49:16-20

Don't Worry

The devil, your enemy, prowls around seeking what he can devour. The devil uses lies, burdens, worry and fear to withhold some of your greatest blessings from Jesus Christ.

Stop listening to his lies and listen to Jesus' truth.

Stop self-prescribing your shortcomings with large portions of your life. That type of prescription is like a horse being lunged with no purpose, going around in mindless circles, achieving no permanent results.

I am humble enough to say that fear makes me stumble more than I'd like to admit, but the Lord gives me constant reminders, just as He did with all His disciples before me. The Lord told Paul time and time again not to fear, not to rebuke him but to reassure him!

So, rest assured, my friend, cast your worries, anxieties, cares, and fears on the Lord because you are His! He loves you; He wants to work it out. He doesn't want you to try to solve your problems on your own, for His way is far greater than yours anyhow.

Every time I climb into the saddle of a new horse

in training, whether it's for the first ride or a tune-up, I remind myself the Lord has got me, no matter what happens. I want the Lord's peace of preparation, not the wiggles of worry.

If the horse bucks, Lord, let me stick to my seat. If my horse trips, Lord, help me to stay balanced and help the horse regain his balance. If we spook, let us go together, Lord. Help me give my horse confidence to be better prepared next time. If my horse rears, Lord, let me dismount with ease and get back on without fear and be filled with Your peace. Lord, I know You've given me this gift to naturally work with one of Your most magnificent creatures, so let me do it to the best of my ability displaying Your goodness, peace, kindness, joy, patience, love, faithfulness, gentleness, and self-control.

Remind me, Lord, that most of these things may never even happen, and I worry about nothing. Reassure me, Lord, to not fear, to look to You, Jesus, for strength. Take any worry, Lord, and give me God-fidence in Your ability to do things far better than I can.

Whatever you face today, ladies and gents, remember the Lord loves you, so cast all the head trash on Him, and watch what He can do. Give it to Jesus. Leave it in His hands. Keep your faith and trust in Him.

Cast all your anxiety on him because he cares for you.

1 PETER 5:7

Seek Passion

Whether in life or in horsemanship, the act of preaching (delivering a message publicly) involves passion, compassion, and a desire to impart truth at the same time.

A person claiming to preach, teach, or instruct, who can speak about these things dispassionately, has no right whatsoever to be in a pulpit or a mentor role; and should never be allowed to enter one.

Watch out for the low prices, shallow services, and lack of truth, compassion, and passion. There are a variety of teachers, trainers, and preachers available as not every single person is on the same level of learning, but make sure you are smart, do your research, and seek the truth to learn correctly to build the right foundation.

> Not many of you should become teachers, my brothers, for you know that we who teach will be judged with greater strictness.
>
> JAMES 3:1

> When the Spirit of truth comes, he will guide you into all the truth, for he will not speak on his own authority, but whatever he hears he will speak, and he will declare to you the things that are to come.
>
> JOHN 16:13

All Scripture is breathed out by God and profitable for teaching, for reproof, for correction, and for training in righteousness, that the man of God may be complete, equipped for every good work.

2 TIMOTHY 3:16-17

Seek the Ultimate Trainer

If your horse is afraid of blackbirds, get them used to eagles. Meaning, prepare your horse with little pressure advancing to extreme pressure, more so than it may ever need to handle, safely, with a purpose, and a little at a time. Read the horse, be aware, and give the horse time to process before pushing him out of his comfort zone. Then be ready when the horse becomes unconfident so he seeks you as the leader. Be ready to redirect him back into confidence and willingness to do his job.

Horses don't get broke at home. You must be willing to put in the time to build a proper foundation, offer confidence in any scenario, and keep safety and fun in mind wherever you go.

Whether in life or in horsemanship, you don't learn by staying locked up in a stall or in your room. You must be willing to brave the scary world. But it's not scary when you have the Ultimate Trainer leading you.

> For God called you to do good, even if it means suffering, just as Christ suffered for you. He is your example, and you must follow in his steps.
>
> 1 PETER 2:21

Running Wild
Isn't Freedom

Mustangs are wild horses that roam free out west across thousands of government lands. Many of these horses live within bands, traveling from place to place. These herds look beautiful running free, with no restrictions, no boundaries, with the idea of a wanderlust spirit and false freedom. Then when these mustangs are rounded up due to excess numbers, that's when the condition of the horse is noticed. The horse is emaciated. Some are covered in scars from defending their position in the herd. Most of the horses have overgrown hooves, broken jaws, broken teeth, and matted hair. Some mares come in pregnant and lose the foals due to a lack of a nutritional diet available. Some have even died out on the range due to scarce resources. Does that really sound like freedom?

Whether in life or in horsemanship, you may see a gorgeous wild horse running free or a person living life without any boundaries. Do not be fooled by these loose ways of life. For horses and humans will live a happier, more fulfilled life by having some type of fence line as a boundary. Boundaries are necessary to teach respect, trust, and faith in One and Only Worthy Handler, who is King Jesus. Boundaries help protect us. Those that are running wild and free may look like they are having the

time of their lives, but that's not the case. These people
that think they are living in freedom are sowing into
mischief instead of sowing into the Spirit. These folks look
like they have all the worldly things, but they are dying
inside. They are discontent, erratic, and unfocused. They
may see boundaries as restrictions, but those two things
are very different. Embrace boundaries, for that leads to
true freedom. Do not sow into the world. Sow into Jesus.
For Jesus gives you fulfillment in yourself and here on
this earth. For the Ultimate Trainer can domesticate the
wildest souls wherever we roam.

> The one who sows to please his sinful nature, from
> that nature will be destruction; the one who sows to
> please the Spirit, from the Spirit will reap eternal life.

GALATIANS 6:8

Frustration Begins
When Knowledge Ends

Refrain from anger and turn from wrath;
do not fret—it leads only to evil.
For evil men will be cut off,
but those who hope in the Lord will inherit the land.

A little while, and the wicked will be no more;
though you look for them, they will not be found.
But the meek will inherit the land
and enjoy great peace.

PSALM 37:8-11

Anger starts where knowledge ends. Whether in life or in horsemanship, do your best never to respond in anger to any situation. For when aggression is displayed, so does foolishness. For the wise, understand the difference between assertiveness and aggression. Pray the Lord opens the ears, hearts, and minds of whoever you are dealing with. Remember, challenges build your faith and character in Christ. He will never give you more than what you can handle. When you feel overwhelmed or lacking in knowledge, seek out Jesus for direction and wisdom. Have a pure heart in whatever you do. Be meek, but don't be a doormat.

Whoever loves discipline loves knowledge, but whoever hates correction is stupid. As you go about your day today, be sincere, be kind, be good, and be humble enough to take some correction. For a good man obtains favor from the Lord.

PROVERBS 12:1-2

Truthful and Correct
Education Is Key

*In the horse world and life in general, statements such as,
"I've been doing this for fifty years" doesn't negate the fact
that someone can do something wrong for fifty years.*

MARTIN BLACK

"I have twenty years of experience riding" doesn't
mean someone has consistently ridden or learned from
knowledgeable mentors. Just because someone is old
doesn't mean they're wise. Watching Clinton Anderson
DVDs, Parelli YouTube, or TikTok will not give you the
experience of training under someone who can point out
things you can do better. Unlike training on our own, it's
very easy to teach our horses the wrong method thinking
our doing it right. So save yourself some heartache and
build a correct foundation on correct education by a
real-life professional. Then, you'll have the tools to do
something's on your own. Just as Olympic riders have
trainers, I choose to have elite professionals as trainers
as well. I make a point to always invest in my future, no
matter who I'm riding with.

I want to ride with people who want to learn just as
much as I do, especially from the horse.

Two things that will never be mastered in life—horses

and Jesus. We must be willing to continue our education in both areas all the rest of our days.

Be careful of those who claim to know it all. Pray that their ears and hearts become open.

Young horses are a lot like babies in Christ. They have a limited attention span. Be mindful to share one topic at a time and keep it simple stupid. Whether horse or human, a baby state of mind isn't developed enough to comprehend a lengthy training session or a college lecture.

You must know the ABCs first, how the letters sound to form words, to then make phrases into sentences.

There are some significant differences between "survival riding" and "horse-man-ship."

Just as there are significant differences in "religion" and having a relationship with Christ Jesus.

> *The capacity to learn is a gift; the ability to learn is a skill; the willingness to learn is a choice.*
>
> BRIAN HERBERT

> The way of fools seems right to them, but the wise listen to advice.
>
> PROVERBS 12:15

A Season of Favor

Freezebrand: #****4053
Rounded up from Green Mountain, Wyoming
(born in holding)

Whether in life or horsemanship, both trails are full of trials and scary circumstances that seem to break us. However, challenges arise to change us, gentle us, and seek out more Christ-like character.

Every single day, we can all relate to having less-than-perfect encounters with tough people, tough horses, and tough situations. How do we handle these moments under pressure? Do we embrace our inner mustang by fleeing for the hills? Do we buck, bite, kick, rear, and whinny every step we take? Do we impatiently paw at the tie post disregarding the goodness our Handler is waiting to offer? Do we walk off from the mounting block, thinking we can successfully navigate the arena of life all on our own? Do we find ourselves bruised, lame, or sore, limping coming into the barn after a tough battle lost playing in the herd?

Have we come to the place where the Ultimate Trainer is desperately needed to change the circumstance? We may think we know everything, but that's a sure sign pride is in the way. Are you seeking restoration and favor? If so, it starts with grace first.

Whether in life or in horsemanship, grace without emotion must be offered to those you love, those you like, those you don't like, and those who you wish liked you. Those folks you're not living at peace with know the Lord can change the circumstances and the hearts of all involved. But you must be willing to call on Jesus and pray over the situation. Many times, I've been faced with unfavorable moments of disaccord, and I praise the Lord for it. Whether it's been a horse or a human, the Lord uses challenges to change us for the better. In my trials, I reach shamelessly for the hand of the Ultimate Trainer. I allow Him to take the lead rope or the reins because I know I can't manage any obstacle course alone. In every tough situation, He changes my perspective and gives me wisdom and knowledge, pushing me out of my comfort zone into a place of trainability. He brings peace to the table. He restores friendships. He kills pride. He elevates humility and covers our lives with goodness and favor. With that being said, I am thankful for the trials because, without them, I wouldn't know the favor of the Lord. As seasons are constantly changing and gray horses go through many phases of color, so should our lives for the better. The more we seek out the Lord, the more He gives, covering us with His grace, His goodness, and His favor. He gives us our hearts' desires, but we must be willing to reach for Him. We must be willing for the Lord to gentle our soul and our situation. Allow Him to restore whatever you face just as He will when He returns to restore His kingdom. Where there were natural enemies, they would all lie together in peace. Here's to a season of favor.

The wolf will live with the lamb, the leopard will lie down with the goat, the calf and the lion and the yearling together; and a little child will lead them.

The cow will feed with the bear, their young will lie down together, and the lion will eat straw like the ox. The infant will play near the hole of the cobra, and the young child put his hand into the viper's nest.

They will neither harm nor destroy on all my holy mountain, for the earth will be full of the knowledge of the LORD as the waters cover the sea.

ISAIAH 11:6-9

Keep Your Love Shades On

What we really believe will be exhibited by our attitudes and actions.

If we're immature in Christ, it'll show. We need to try to keep a tight rein on our tongue and the words we type. A fool has no control of their tongue (Proverbs 15:2).

Those who judge will also be judged (Matthew 7:2).

If you seek after Christ to grow in Him, that, too, will show. If we're humble and love Christ, that will show. True love of Christ is being obedient to His voice and all His laws. No matter how hateful the world is towards us, keep pushing forward. For even Jesus was persecuted and hated by those in His own town, by His own family (John 15:18, Matthew 13:57).

Never hate those who hate you, pray for those who persecute, pray for blessings over their life. Be the better person. For you are a child of God, so act like it.

Haters are going to hate. But keep your love shades on.

You can only speak to those who are willing. For

those who think they know it all, they will be their own stumbling block.

> The Lord is faithful, and He will strengthen and protect you from the evil one.

2 THESSALONIANS 3:3

Pray for those who lack knowledge, who can't see the truth, who are lost in their fleshly desires, and who can't see beyond your news feed.

There's more to life than comparison. We each have our own purpose in Christ if we're willing to listen to Him. If we're willing to work for it.

Stand firm in His truth, and know the Lord has your back. He has not brought you this far to fail. He is leading you into greatness. Focus on all the positive He does in your life.

Hold your head up high, and adjust your crown, for you are a child of the Most High.

The Lord will crush your enemies. He has already won. You are not alone.

Fear your Father, respect Him, and have no fear in this world because you belong to the Almighty King Jesus.

Actions speak louder than words.

Keep on keeping on.

You are a son and a daughter of the King.

He is the truth, the light, and He will set you free.

Smile in the face of the wicked because the Son lives in you.

You Have Already
Won the Battle

When you are in a situation where you feel underhanded, remember that is when you need to cling to Christ the most.

Fleshly emotions are deceiving. Christ-like attributes are not.

Continue to share your God-given talents and focus on Jesus. You are not to be a people pleaser. You are to be a Jesus pleaser. Regardless of what people may think of you, keep doing what you're doing for the Lord.

Your strength comes from the Lord. Your knowledge comes from the Lord. When your God-given wisdom is underhanded, be gracious to those who persecute you. It's hard, I know, but shut up and do it! Cling to that word to help you.

Be the example of Christ even under fire. Be at peace with everyone. Allow the Lord to intervene, take over the situation, and restore peace and joy.

When you are misjudged, falsely accused, slighted, or underappreciated, the impulse to bolster your personal reputation is a powerful temptation. While pursuing truth is certainly noble, the all-consuming desire to be right—

to trumpet your side of the story—can quickly become a stumbling block in the pursuit of greater influence. Have quiet integrity.

Don't be a stumbling block to those you influence.

You don't need the last word. You have nothing to prove, be humble, bridle your tongue, and let the Lord work.

You can't fix this alone. You can't make things right. Only Jesus can. His yoke is easy, and His burden is light.

> If it is possible, as far as it depends on you, live at peace with everyone.
>
> ROMANS 12:18

Don't allow the fleshly fiery darts to weigh you down. For you have already won the battle, for Jesus lives in you, so let His light shine.

Enemies Are Sent to Increase You

For the ones who plan wickedly will be put to shame. Don't complain about your enemies. The Lord will use them to bless you abundantly.

Keep your eyes on Jesus, don't give the devil any power to distract you from the blessings in front of you, and remember the Lord already has a plan for your life, far better than what you could ever imagine!

David would only be known as a shepherd boy if it weren't for Goliath. Goliath was strategically placed in David's path, not to defeat him but to promote him. Without Goliath, David would have never taken the throne. Again, don't complain about your enemies. It may look like a setback, but really, it's a setup for God to get you to your throne (1 Samuel chapter 17).

After all, God could have used King Saul to promote David. Saul had the authority. He could have moved on. Saul's heart told him to promote that young man, but God chose to bless David, not through his friends but through his enemies.

Sometimes, the Lord will put enemies in our lives to keep us stirred up. He'll allow critics, doubters, discouragers, and even some haters, so when we feel tired and want to give up, we'll keep pressing forward, shaking it off not because we feel like it but because we don't want to give your enemies the joy of seeing you defeated. Not out of spite, not out of pride, it's a holy determination. The Lord uses that negative to keep us spiritually motivated.

That's why we don't have to play up to people. Try to convince them to like us. The ones that are trying to push us down, He can use them to push us up. It's interesting when David defeated Goliath. You never hear any more about Goliath. Goliath was created for David's purpose. Part of his destiny was to establish who David was. Just as God has divine connections lined up for you, people to encourage you and push you forward, He's also lined up people that will try to stop you, discourage you, and try to make you look bad. There are Goliath's ordained to come across your path, not to stop you but to establish you. When you overcome it, you will not only step into a new level of your destiny, but everyone around you will see the favor of God is on your life.

So, when people are talking about you, trying to make you look bad, trying to push you down, or they're dragging your name through the arena dirt. Don't worry, God hears them. Those people are putting you in a position for the Lord to bless you in a greater way. You don't have to straighten them out. Don't fight battles that don't matter, stay in peace, and God will use your enemies to bless you. Some of the favor that you're seeing, some of the good breaks you've had, it didn't happen because of you.

It happened because of those people that tried to stop you. They put you in a position for promotion. I thank the Lord for my friends, but I've learned to thank Him for my enemies as well. Without the murmuring, that man may not have been healed; without Goliath, David would have never taken his throne; without Judas, Jesus wouldn't have been resurrected from the grave. You need to see every enemy, so to speak, every disappointment, every betrayal in this new light: it's not sent to defeat you. It's sent to increase you. God can use your critics to promote you. God has all kinds of ways to get you to where you're supposed to be. He knows how to take what was meant for your harm and turn it around and use it to your advantage.

The Lord will make your enemies your footstool. Anything that comes against you: the persecution, the betrayal, the disappointment; if you'll stay in faith instead of it being a stumbling block to take you down, God will use it as a stepping stone to take you higher (Psalm 110:1).

Glory of Jehovah Jireh

Freezebrand: #****2573
Rounded up from HMA unknown;
born in holding, Teterville, Kansas

Words are not the same as they were. The world and
the flesh find many ways to twist and turn simple terms
to fit the needs of what they want it to believe. One word
can have many translations, and the irony of it—it can
still be misinterpreted.

This is why having a relationship with Christ is so
important. When we have a real and invested relationship
with Jesus, the Holy Spirit reveals truth, understanding,
and the real definition of words we see to understand.

The Greek meaning of "glory"—*doxazo* (verb)—
to magnify, praise. Ascribing honor to God and
acknowledging Him and His being, attributes, and actions.

"Let your light so shine before men, that they may
see your good works and glorify your Father in heaven"
(Matthew 5:16; Romans 15:6; Galatians 1:24; 1 Peter 4:16).

Jehovah Jireh means "the Lord will provide," referring
to the undeniable faith that Abraham had the day the
Lord instructed Him to sacrifice a burnt offering, which
was his son, but God! Before Abraham followed through,
the Lord told Abraham he would provide a lamb. I'm

paraphrasing here. In the final hour, an angel appeared. Abraham looked up and saw a ram in the thicket! I can only imagine what relief Abraham felt. This event, though, shows Abraham's faith and obedience to the Lord.

So, without further ado, in honor of the Lord and my father-in-law, who was faithful to the Lord Jesus until the very end, giving God all the glory, praising Jesus through His pain and suffering here on earth, leading to the provision of my father-in-law being promoted to heaven and made whole.

I present the newest member of our blessed herd, "Glory of Jehovah Jireh," Glory (for short).

She was a rescue, taken in by Pasture Pals ER in 2012. She was roughly 750 pounds when Alex and her team seized her. She was extremely beaten up and had many battle scars to date. She was burnt and beaten with a chain. A halter had grown into her face, she had overgrown hooves, and she was so emaciated the mare's pregnancy was a surprise the following spring. Long story short, or should I say long story long... Glory has landed in a soft spot here.

Glory will be retrained here at TOFF. She will eventually be integrated into one of our programs that will best suit her horsenality. Until then, a slow start into refreshers on handling, ground manners, and confidence building. I believe no matter the age of a horse, even at nineteen years young (such as Glory), there can be a future for any horse. It's just all based on how much work the handler is willing to put in. I'm all in Glory! And so is the TOFF crew. Thank you, Alex, for the blessing of the sweet, sassy, drafty mustang to come to her new forever home. Praise the Lord for Glory of Jehovah Jireh. One of many blessings in our life.

Don't Neigh About It;
Pray About It

Jesus is the best example of having a prayer-filled life.
Every moment Jesus was faced with trials and triumphs,
He prayed. Prayer is a Christian's lifeline to hear the
Father's voice and to obtain peace in the famine. Prayer
connects us to our Father. Without having a committed
prayer life, communication and relationships will be weak.
When we're faced with an overload of problems, we should
seek Christ out in prayer instead of complaining about it.
Just like every morning, I'm greeted with neighs, nickers,
and brays. All the horses (and the donkey) are waiting at
their feed pans impatiently to receive their breakfast. They
are continuously communicating with each other. They are
making it known that the glorified lunch lady isn't feeding
fast enough. Their neighs of complaints don't stop until
the gift of their breakfast is placed into eating reach. The
peace of having a full belly hushes the neighs and brays as
they've been provided what was needed.

Whether in life or in horsemanship, the Lord
provides all that's needed when there's an open line of
communication. We can't discern His voice if we're not
talking to Him. We should be bringing every petition
and request to Him for guidance, provision, and peace.
We should be seeking Him every morning to fill our

bellies full with the Bread of Life instead of impatiently waiting at the feed pan. Rather, seek the Lord out in prayer. Jesus prayed all the time, and so should we. If we want to grow our understanding in Christ and obtain a peace that surpasses all understanding, seek the Father out. If we want to hear our Father's voice, we must be willing to speak with Him. We can't expect to have a friendship without ever speaking to our friends. Instead of complaining about our problems, much like the neighing and braying of impatience, seek the Lord out and pray.

> The Lord is near. Do not be anxious about anything, but in everything, by prayer and petition, with thanksgiving, present your requests to God. And the peace of God, which transcends all understanding, will guard your hearts and your minds in Christ Jesus.

> PHILIPPIANS 4:5-7

For Wide Is the Gate

A horse is uniquely made in His Father's eyes for a purpose. He gives each horse different attributes and personalities created just for each one.

He established the ability of the horse long ago, engrained their natural instincts, to show His great power and grace, never wavering in trouble, but only to react the same; either fight or flight.

As humans, the Lord has uniquely made us all in His own image, giving us each our own identities in Christ. When we choose to live by His Word, fully embracing His instructions of scriptures, we, too, can respond consistently, as a horse does, to fight or flee in situations we're put in. We are to fight the good fight and flee from provocativeness, never intentionally dance with the devil. Instead of responding as a human, emotionally, speaking from our flesh, we must speak to the evil one with the words of Jesus, for that is the name even demons tremble at.

We must seek completely after Jesus Christ, filling our spirit with His guidance and building our foundation constantly through His leadership.

As a horse trainer, when I'm working with horses, I ask each equine questions to see what they're capable of, putting pressure on them to see how they react, which proves to them I can be a worthy leader. The Lord knows what He's doing. He doesn't need to prove He is a worthy leader. However, He continues to pour out and show up in all of our lives. He willingly shows us that He is worthy, that He is consistent, never fleeing like a horse or human would. He is always fighting for us, no matter how unqualified we may feel. The Lord knows we are capable. He has a unique purpose for you and everyone else who is willing to embrace Him and follow His steps. Never leaving us or forsaking us and holding our hand through it all.

A dorsal stripe is a thin, narrow stripe running atop the back, center through the widest parts of the horse.

> For wide is the gate and broad is the road that leads to destruction, and many enter through it. But small is the gate and narrow the road that leads to life, and only few find it.
>
> MATTHEW 7:13-14

We must strive to stay on that narrow path of everlasting love and faith.

The Ultimate Trainer
Refines the Basics

You never stop refining the basics, and a true horseman knows this. So if you truly learn to refine the basics, your work with horses can look boring, and as if the horse doesn't have any trouble, because you didn't put him in trouble in the first place. That is the whole point of learning to handle horses well—not to show off, but to have something real to offer horses.

AMY SKINNER

Whether on the ground or on horseback, a true horseman refines the basics. When it's evident, the horse will display softness, relaxation in the face and body, and offer willingness. The horse will be seeking you for comfort, confidence, and leadership versus looking to his herd mates. Signs that you've skipped some basic steps and principles with your horse are a high head, a bracey neck, a hollow body, a tight tail, a horse that backs up when asked to go forward, and a horse that spooks sideways or bolts in fear. These are all signs of diseases of domestication. When our priorities are above the welfare of the horse, we tend to disregard signs of illness.

When those signs are evident, a real horseman doesn't just push the horse through the fear to get what they want. A real horseman takes the horse into consideration. A real horseman isn't focused on their goal or the owner's goal but treats the horse in front of them. A real horseman keeps the horse's welfare in mind.

There are millions of trainers available, much like millions of religions available, and it's hard to discern truth and authenticity in it all. We should be looking past the "mustang gentlers" and "horse whisperers." We should look beyond those who claim to know it all or the ones who spotlight their blue ribbons. Look past the titles advertised and the need to be recognized. A real horseman can easily be spotted through all the smoke and lights. A real horseman's work will look boring, constantly repeating and teaching foundational exercises, but the evidence is available in the horses and humans around them.

The next time you are around a trainer, do you see the qualities of a horseman? Or are they going through the motions to get results?

Just as the Lord continues to refine my basics, I do the same with every horse I work with.

Basics are a blessing. Whether in life or in horsemanship, we must learn the basics first. We must learn the ABCs before we can form words into sentences. Our horses must understand basic principles with pure confidence in my leadership. When that basic principle is mastered every single time, the door is opened to willingness to offer greater basic concepts. Allow the Ultimate Trainer to keep refining the basics.

See, I have refined you, though not as silver; I have tested you in the furnace of affliction.

ISAIAH 48:10

Watered Down Truth

The idea of sharing your faith in Christ is not forcing it on anyone. You will immediately lose interest in that person, just as a horse will lose interest in you if you try to force them to do anything.

When you are driven by fleshly emotions and desires, you lose focus on what Christ really has to offer you. To share the love of Christ should be reflected in your daily life out in the world.

The Lord Jesus offers acceptance of you just the way you are. That doesn't mean making excuses for your sin and keeping on living it. He forgives us all of our sins daily (Colossians 3:1–17).

All the Lord wants is for us to live by His Word. He wants us to follow His commands and for us to reach our full potential in Christ. Nothing in this world can bless you like being a child of Christ. The Lord will turn your confusion into understanding. He brings clarity to the mind. You just have to be willing to seek Him out, listen to Him, open up your Bible, and apply His Word to your heart. If you can't be obedient to His Word, you do not truly love the Lord. A profession of love doesn't produce obedience. Love is keeping His laws.

The world loves to water down truth. Don't be influenced

by those who water down His truth (Colossians 2:8).

Whether it's faith or horsemanship, there is a basis of integrity for everything. Don't just go along with something because it "sounds" right. You should really understand the words you're hearing. Don't be fooled by false teachings. Be wary of philosophies that do not exalt the One True Christ.

Lip service is just noise with no purpose.

Just as I am committed to each horse I work with, asking for obedience based on truth, I am just as committed to my Father of truth. I show my love by being obedient. I'm constantly asking Him for direction and for His guidance daily. I strive each day to make myself better for Him, just as I do with each horse I work with. The Lord Jesus gives me strength every day to fight the attacks of the devil. He is my guard, my shield, and He protects me from the principalities of darkness.

Whether in the valley or on the mountaintop, I am never alone. He is always by my side, lifting me up in truth and in Spirit. I am a child of the King. I am a conqueror in Christ Jesus (Romans 8:31–38).

Mentoring

Our goal as mentors is to minister. Mentoring shouldn't be a way to meet our needs for significance but to walk with others as they grow and become like Christ. Our goal as a mentor should never be to shape our mentors into our image but to encourage them to bear God's image more fully.

God brings about change, not us. Mentoring is not our opportunity to implement our agenda in the life of another person. It is our opportunity to walk with another person as God shapes them into His image. Shed His light, share His love, and allow the Lord to intervene, convict, change, and grow those around you. We are to be willing vessels to plant gospel seeds. Then allow the Holy Spirit to draw the person.

Whether in life or in your horsemanship, an educated mentor will teach, "Do as I say, as well as do what I do," NOT one or the other. Whatever task is at hand, from grooming a horse to saddling to leading, be the example in action and in word. If we can't demonstrate what we speak, we lack discipline, experience, and knowledge. Be a positive example, whether in private or in public, for someone is ALWAYS watching.

> I myself am convinced, my brothers and sisters, that you yourselves are full of goodness, filled with knowledge and competent to instruct one another.
>
> ROMANS 15:14

Lessons from Difficult Horses

Some of the most difficult horses (and people) will teach us more than we could ever dream. When our confidence is shaken, take it not as a warning but as a reminder to learn and grow. Pay attention more to the small things. Details matter. Training horses is no different than life; you have triumphant days reaching the top of the mountain and other days where you feel out at the lowest point in the valley. But don't give up or give in! For the blessing is right around the corner.

Some may say I'm stupid. Some say my dreams are too big to happen. But I know who my Father is. I have more faith than a mustard seed. I have many neigh-sayers around me, but I also have amazing people who support me, my dreams, and my beautiful ministry. I am blessed with an amazing husband who pushes me, even when I want to throw in the towel.

For our success goes to the One and Only King Jesus. Even when I get kicked down (or kicked square in my chest), I will get back up stronger, fiercer, as the lamb and the lion are within me.

The Lord is within me, guiding me, giving me strength.

So, today's encouragement for all of you who are a

weary and heavy burden—do not lose hope, for the Lord never leaves. He never forsakes you, just reach out to Him, and He will answer.

> When my spirit grows faint within me it is you who know my way...

PSALM 142:3A

Search for Understanding

Common misconception that during training, when a horse is offered to check out a training flag, carrot stick, saddle pad, saddle, etc., is it's being offered to smell. When training horses, you must search to understand the following:

What to do?
How to do it?
And why you're doing it?

If we're simply going through the motions because it was seen on YouTube once, it's most likely not learned correctly, and the results will end up with a confused, frustrated horse.

Knowing the "why" should motivate us to steward our horses in the best way possible. Go beyond the "basics." Stewarding is much like being an ambassador, as in respectfully representing and taking care of your horse. How are you taking care of your horse? Not physically but mentally. Horses are a direct reflection of their stewards. They will mirror their handler's knowledge or lack of it. You get out what you put in.

By having a true understanding of the horse and a correct frame of mind, in this case, the horse uses his whiskers to FEEL and not smell whatever training tool is presented to him. Allow your horse to be curious. Never knock the curiosity out of a horse, as that will result in low confidence and mistrust. Allow them to feel with their whiskers and lips, but of course, set boundaries where biting is not a go-to result. Take every opportunity to set your horse up for success. Allow your horse to process every request by knowing the telltale subtle signs after a "ask," i.e., lowering its head below its withers, licking its lips, yawning, resting a leg, and blinking, which means thinking.

When you become frustrated and a 1 percent change isn't produced, find a trainer and mentor to learn from. Frustration begins where knowledge ends. Remember— don't worry, think less, and have fun!

> Therefore I tell you, do not worry about your life, what you will eat or drink; or about your body, what you will wear. Is not life more important than food, and the body more important than clothes?
>
> MATTHEW 6:25

Correction Is Love

As a trainer, I fine-tune my horses just as the Lord fine-tunes me. I correct them because I love them. I do my best to build up faith and trust in each horse, proving that I can be a worthy leader. I never leave them stranded or abandoned when faced with obstacles in the arena of life. When times get tough, I want every horse I work with to seek me out instead of zoning in on their natural instinct to get out of dodge.

Whether in life or in my horsemanship, it's a never-ending process of Jesus teaching me new things. I am open to correction by my Father. I want Him to make me better. Just as I want each horse I work with to be more of an educated partner.

The Lord opens my mind to think more like Him daily. Christ Jesus allows me to gain wisdom and knowledge in His truth. These things do not grow without a right relationship and a correct foundation built on salvation. Salvation comes from Jesus. For every obstacle I'm faced with, Jesus sticks right by my side, guiding me with His unfailing hand. He never leaves me or forsakes me. He stays consistent, building up my faith in Him. For He corrects me because He loves me. For He is the worthiest Trainer. He continues to guide me through the arena of life, making a way through the toughest obstacles.

My son, do not despise the Lord's discipline and do not resent his rebuke, because the Lord disciplines those he loves, as a father the son he delights in. Blessed is the man who finds wisdom, the man who gains understanding, for she is more profitable than silver and yields better returns than gold. She is more precious than rubies; nothing you desire can compare with her.

PROVERBS 3:11-15

For wisdom and knowledge is a gift from Jesus Christ.

Level of Commitment

Instead of having a prideful mentality, the human set out to teach the horse. What If only we allowed ourselves to learn from the horse? What if we accepted them as the teacher and ourselves as the student? A student of the horse humbly accepting change and awareness, just as the Lord offers to us. What if we offered the same act of giving? What if we offered trust to our horse as the Lord extends to us?

What if we kept going when we didn't feel like it? What if we knew the breakthrough was right around the corner? What if we stopped focusing on fear and worry? What if we pressed on when it was too hard? What if we had a complete focus to bring our goal to fruition?

Instead of saying no to the challenges and distractions, what if we constantly said yes? What if we embraced the challenge to change?

Whether in life or in horsemanship, what if we truly were honest with ourselves about our level of commitment (and our level of knowledge)? What does our commitment look like to our spouse, our horse, our friends, and our acquaintances?

Does it reflect the commitment to change, or does it scream mundane disobedience?

A horse sees past our disappearing acts and our lack of commitment. Ultimately, it will be revealed each time we work with him. We will have a far better relationship with the Lord and our horse if we show up daily and constantly put forth effort and change, regardless of the circumstances.

It's never too late to put forth responsibility leading to a change in Christ.

We should have a level of commitment that reflects closeness, loyalty, reliability, and devotion. Go beyond being a passenger and seek out a partnership.

A quality relationship isn't showing up to the barn once in a blue moon or attending holiday church services.

A quality relationship is the exact opposite. Stop normalizing the magician's acts. Stop making excuses. Stop quitting on yourself, your horse, and Christ.

Keep your eyes focused on Jesus. Stay focused on Him, and He will see you through the peace and the chaos.

Don't quit when it's boring, challenging, or discouraging. Call on King Jesus for encouragement and direction. Be committed to the Father by seeking after Him in every moment of weakness. Seek Jesus in prayer and in His Word.

Be reminded that our level of commitment may change, but His never will. He is always there waiting for us to be devoted and obedient. Desire to do His will.

Commit your way to the Lord; trust in him and he will do this: He will make your righteousness shine like dawn, the justice of your cause like the noonday sun.

PSALM 37:5-6

Be Drawn by the Handler

Basic principles are oftentimes forgotten or overlooked in the process of training a horse. We forget the importance of details and simple tasks such as catching and haltering. We have motives and direct line objectives solidifying our predator instincts working with a prey animal, such as a horse. Even describing the acquisition of our horse above, many important details were left out. Before we even think about putting a halter and a lead rope on our horse, what if we first thought like a partner instead of a predator? A horse is drawn to other horses because they willingly come together. Every horse in a herd has a specific role to defend, find food, find water, reproduce, and survive. Hundreds of horses come together to form one herd. Just like all members in Christ form one body of Christ, working together for the upbuilding of His kingdom. We are all assigned specific roles to protect, build up, and grow the kingdom of Christ.

But first, before we can build up one another, we must be drawn by the Holy Spirit. Before we can catch and halter our horse, our horse must be drawn by us. When we have "draw," we create a willing curiosity in our horse to come to us. We create an honest concept for our horse to join up with our herd. We are offering a path of hope and correction for our horse paved with comfort, safety, truth, and leadership. What do dishonest training techniques look like? Hiding the halter from the horse, sliding the halter underneath or in front of the horse's face where they can't see it, distracting them with cookies and slipping the halter on while their face is in a bucket, slinging the lead rope around the horse's neck with an "I gotcha" attitude, roping the horse to get the halter on; well, you get the idea as the list goes on and on. Generally, these techniques create hard-to-catch horses. These techniques get quick results and may work for a time, but these concepts were obtained dishonestly by the handler and unwillingly from the horse. Without a transparent curiosity, why should our horse come to us? What if we enlighten our minds and go back to the basics before haltering? Do we have a willing partner drawn to us? When we step into the horse's stall or work area, do they pull at our heart? Do they have a desire to be with us?

Whether in life or in horsemanship, we can only be caught and haltered when we have been drawn by our Handler. For only the Holy Spirit can draw us closer to Christ. The Spirit makes us aware of our sinful nature and our need for a Savior. The Holy Spirit works in us by pulling at our hearts. He then changes our desires to build up and edify His kingdom. The Lord honestly and openly draws us to the Holy Spirit before He catches us; we should offer the same to our horse. Then together, honestly, we can be drawn down a path of hope, salvation, and correction paved with security, safety, growth, and truth.

"Stop grumbling among yourselves," Jesus answered. "No one can come to me unless the Father who sent me draws him, and I will raise him up at the last day."

JOHN 6:43-44

A Good Trainer

A good trainer is committed to putting endless hours
into fine-tuning their horses. There's no need to
micromanage. We must allow them to make choices,
and if it wasn't exactly what we asked, we ask again and
correct if needed.

A good trainer corrects from love.

A good trainer wants to see their horse succeed and build
them up for a long life of happiness built on the right
relationship of confidence and trust.

A good trainer offers security in their leadership.

A good trainer offers comfort in their leadership instead
of the horse seeking comfort from treats, hay, or their
herd mates.

A good trainer offers security in their leadership.

A good trainer has the horse's best interest at heart.

Just as the Lord does the same for us. He is the
Ultimate Trainer who's committed to fine-tuning us. He
corrects me with love, grace, and firmness. He has our
best interest at heart. He disciplines the ones He loves
(Hebrews 12:6).

The Lord Jesus has our best interest at heart, never

guiding us into a situation that we can't handle. We must have complete trust and faith in the Lord, just as I seek this from the horses I request the deepest followership from.

I must display willingness to receive willingness.

For the Lord gives wisdom, and from His mouth come knowledge and understanding.

It is not my wisdom. It is His.

Champions Have Humility

A by-product of sincere humility is trust, respect, and security in whatever role the Lord puts you in.

Authentic humility and love inspire us to put God before everything else, no matter what the price. When you have an open mind and attitude to learn every moment, it will show in your work.

I put the Lord first in all I do, including my gifts as a horse trainer. Just as the Lord wants me to humbly accept His corrections and directions, leading to growth, I ask the same from every horse I work with. When you build on a proper foundation of faith and trust, holes are avoided, and there's willingness from your equine to confidently follow you anywhere.

Where the Lord wants every person to humbly accept His wisdom to follow Him every day, I strive to offer the same thing to my horses. I strive for progression, not perfection. I establish in each equine that I can be a trusted leader, just as Christ is for me. For I am far from perfect, but thank the Lord for His grace and the Holy Spirit in me to do better than the day before.

> Therefore, as God's chosen people, holy and dearly loved, clothe yourselves with compassion, kindness, humility, gentleness and patience.
>
> COLOSSIANS 3:12

Questions for Your Mentor

When starting out or continuing your education as a horseman or horsewoman, ask questions about who you're considering. Don't just look at certifications that rarely anyone asks. Yes, those can be helpful, but if you can't physically see results, then there is most likely a lack of commitment. I am bringing horses because they do not leave the same as they arrived. They are transformed. They leave with better skills. Clients get what they seek, an improved relationship and better savvy skills. If you take the time it takes, it'll take less time. Avoid taking shortcuts for the cheapest source; you get what you pay for.

Ask yourself some of these questions for prospective trainers:

Is safety always in mind?
Are helmets required for youth and greenhorns?
Is the property clean and inviting?
Is their philosophy of horses shared? What discipline and specialty is focused on? Are horses just tools or magical creatures?
Is everything consistently clean? Bathroom, water troughs, horses?
Do the horses offer themselves to visitors? Are they inquisitive, or are they resigned?
What do they feed? Hay is important.
When something goes wrong, who gets the blame?

"Find someone who can inspire you and make the magic live. Safety is always a first consideration. If it's not, leave. Have fun! Choose an instructor who inspires you. Choose an instructor who matches or compliments your personality" (author unknown).

Even as a trainer myself, I have a trainer. You can't grow without having mentors. Pick ones that you would aspire to be like. Pick someone with positive values and a hard work ethic. Someone that will push you. If you're not being pushed out of your comfort zone, you're not growing.

> And let us consider how we may spur one another on toward love and good deeds. Let us not give up meeting together, as some are in the habit of doing, but let us encourage one another—and more as you see the Day approaching.
>
> HEBREWS 10:24-25

Feral Versus *Wild*

The definition of "feral" is oftentimes referred to horses that were once domesticated and influenced by humans but ran away from ownership or care and escaped a domestic lifestyle to revert to their wild ways. These horses have been exposed to horse-human relationships. Maybe some of it was good or bad. Maybe these horses had a poor environment with no exposure to progression in training. Maybe these horses craved a human relationship, but they weren't tended to or cultivated to appreciate boundaries, trust, and the right relationship. Maybe these horses were exposed to false teachings and false leadership, dressed in cookies, lies, deception, sedation, or lack of knowledge.

The definition of "wild" is also oftentimes referred to when talking about horses; wild means to be untamed and untouched, having no familiarity, care, or cultivation from humans. These horses have never seen a human and have never experienced a right relationship. These horses have no influence from humans and have no knowledge that we can be worthy leaders. These horses have never been exposed to the goodness of truthful and transparent leadership, showered with boundaries of safety, trust, love, gentleness, kindness, hope, and purpose.

Whether in life or in horsemanship, if we are in a feral state, having once known the Ultimate Trainer, we've been misguided and mistreated. We may find ourselves reverting to our wild ways now that we can never lose our faith, but we can lose the ability to mature in Christ. When we find ourselves falling away from Christ, don't lose heart. Rededicate your life. Hold on fast to daily repentance, His Word, pray, and turn away from old feral ways. Stay focused on the road of domestication, leading to the Ultimate Trainer.

As Christians, when we are presented with an opportunity to share our hope and faith in Christ with a wild soul, someone who has never been exposed to the Master Horseman's salvation, goodness, love, humility, and kindness, do so in a manner of gracious deliverance. Share the good news and plant seeds in such a way these wild souls crave what they see. May they crave the right relationship you have with Jesus, pulling them out of a state of wilderness.

Whether feral or wild, it starts with being drawn by the Holy Spirit. Salvation must come first to be able to receive peace, joy, and a purpose. We must constantly cultivate our relationship with Christ, put forth the effort, never give up, and keep turning away from our feral ways. Do not abandon your faith when it looks rough. Do not be deceived. When the trail ahead is full of obstacles, stay focused on Master Horseman, as He's leading you to blessings that are right around the bend.

The Spirit clearly says that in later times some will

abandon the faith and follow deceiving spirits and things taught by demons. Such teachings come through hypocritical liars, whose consciences have been seared as with a hot iron.

1 TIMOTHY 4:1-2

Victory Over the Vices

Horses and humans are oftentimes products of their environment. Sometimes, we don't realize how much of an impact our surroundings have on our character. We are constantly flooded with information to sway us to rely on ourselves. Oftentimes, we create a low-quality environment for ourselves and our horses. This type of environment provides no purpose and "useless" actions. This is when diseases of domestication are born from a less-than-fabulous living situation. Diseases of domestication are referred to as vices. Vices are unwanted behaviors or bad habits developed to burn energy. Oftentimes, these bad habits are labeled as being derived from boredom, but that's not the case. So, what happens when we limit ourselves to isolation? We start to react with vices physically or mentally. A horse in isolation without proper food, hay, and minerals, either in a stall or a paddock alone, will demonstrate cribbing, pacing, weaving, head bobbing, windsucking, kicking, biting, and rearing, and may come off as "dull" or "spooky." Now horses aren't humans, and humans aren't horses. Meaning we must be aware and careful not to project human emotions onto horses. Characterizing is vastly different as emotions aren't attached.

A human in isolation without proper food, positive influences, or turnout time will develop physical and mental vices. Some humans may develop "useless" habits by drinking, smoking, indulging in drugs, money, sex, gambling, or committing crimes. An underdeveloped environment can also produce vices such as slothfulness, pride, self-mutilation, anxious tendencies, pacing, confusion, wickedness, and a lack of motivation, and may come off as "dull," "checked out," or "erratic."

When we are responsible for these vices by creating the perfect petri dish for these diseases to breed, how can we change it? How can we overcome these diseases of domestication?

Whether horse or human, we shouldn't try to stop these unwanted behaviors, but we should try to prevent them by providing a better environment. When vices arise, that's when we should step in to make an immediate change. Don't ignore it, don't try to fill the void on your own, don't make excuses, don't over-emotionalize, stop feeding the flesh, and allow the Lord to step in so you can have victory over these vices.

We must allow the Ultimate Trainer to come into our territory. We must allow Him to increase our environment. He will change these "useless" actions to purposeful ones. The Lord will take away our moral faults and wicked behaviors and transform them into virtues leading to good character. When the Master Horseman changes us, our environment changes around us, and our vices subside. Then the Lord instills in us a purpose providing useful actions such as good habits wrapped in kindness, courage, self-control, modesty, wisdom, knowledge, awareness, patience, love, joy, hospitality, and more than we can imagine. Whether in life or in horsemanship, stay encouraged, my friend, as Master Horseman is near. He's readily available to give you victory over the vices. He's able to heal the diseases of domestication. He has a purpose and a plan for each one of us. We just have to be obedient and willing to lay it all down at His feet and follow the Ultimate Trainer.

> For everyone born of God overcomes the world. This is the victory that has overcome the world, even our faith. Who is it that overcomes the world? Only he who believes that Jesus is the Son of God.
>
> 1 JOHN 5:4-5

Why the Wait Is Important

It's very easy to fall into a routine of complacency each day we are presented with. Complacency is wrapped with carelessness, laziness, impatience, doubt, pride, self-satisfaction, self-assurance, self-reliance, and a lack of strictness. Society constantly floods our minds with self-fulfillment. We should have received all our desires yesterday, plus a gratuity. If that isn't far from the truth. We want the boss's job, but we don't want to work our way to it. We want more responsibility but don't care to complete simple tasks. We want to make six figures with little to no work ethic. We want a microwave relationship with our friends, our spouses, and our horses but have no desire to maintain it. We want a sense of being, a full-filled purpose, but the desire to grow and change isn't wanted. We want to rush through the waiting period when we're not ready to receive a specific revelation or blessing. Let's reflect for a moment.

All the thoughts above are selfishly motivated and can very easily be changed, but it starts with awareness first. We can't be promoted to our true purpose without being fully committed to Jesus. We can't get where we want to be without a waiting period to be transformed into where we need to be. We must be willing to be all in, reliant on the Lord in the waiting period. If we continue the road of self-reliance, the Lord will postpone our purpose. If we can't be trusted with little, we can't be trusted with much. If we try to rush through the wait, we will miss the opportunity to grow. How do we pull ourselves out of a state of complacency? How do we get rid of self-doubt and pride? How do we get rid of comparison, jealousy, the fear of rejection, failure, and loneliness? How can we be trained to our full potential? How can we increase our level of commitment in the waiting period? How can we be passionate about our true purpose? It all starts with Jesus.

Whether in life or in horsemanship, nothing can be rushed through and obtained well. While impatience can most certainly get the job done, we will eventually have to return to the basics for a redo, as it was a job poorly done. Waiting is important. It provides experiences to promote good responses. It builds our confidence and our trust in whom we believe. We should be looking for subtle signs of relaxation leading to softness and confidence. When we are focused on the end goal, we miss the call to change. An explosion typically happens when we are unresponsive to the gentle nudges of correction from the Ultimate Trainer. Even then, it's never too late to get back on track on the path of transformative training. In whatever we are set forth to do, be still. Wait for the signs of relaxation, a low head, a lick and chew, some yawning, maybe a propped leg, and a willing spirit to be drawn to the Handler. Don't rush to throw the saddle on without proper preparation. We can't have testimonies without tests. We must embrace the challenges. We must allow Master Horseman to bring us to awareness, to change us, to soften us, to shield us from complacency and impatience. We must remind ourselves we can't get through the arena of life alone, but we can successfully ride through it with the Ultimate Trainer. Don't lose heart. Joyfully endure the waiting period, for there is a time for everything. And whatever opportunity we are presented with, do it well, even if it's for five minutes. For when we can be trusted with little, we can be trusted with much.

> Whatever your hand finds to do, do it with all your might, for in the grave, where you are going, there is neither working nor planning nor knowledge nor wisdom.

> ECCLESIASTES 9:10

Wild to Worthy

Oftentimes, the gentling of a wild mustang is referred to as the process of "wild to mild" or "wild to willing," meaning we are taking this once unhandled spicy mustang to a place of less heat. We started out with a Carolina reaper, moved our way down to scotch bonnet, then jalapeno, in hopes of getting to bell pepper. All the while giving the spicy stung basic handling skills according to what horse is presented to us each time we work with it. The "wild to willing" process takes steps a bit further, progressing in hand skills and starting under saddle, still on the journey of lowering the heat, but all the while keeping the mustangs' spirit intact, providing boundaries of the right relationship leading to willingness. We don't water down the heat to make it less offensive or more digestible. We offer truth and correction and point our mustang back to safety, in us, in times of discomfort. Before the gentling process took place, we were unaware of the goodness these mustangs possess.

They are considered lost, pests, throwaways, runaways, worthless, thieves of the lands, and broom tails.

Their parents were rebels. Their brothers were strays.

Before the gentling process from Master Horseman, our parents were strays, falling away from the truth told by Jesus, enticed by the forbidden fruit, sweet like a bell pepper. When it was tasted, we brought in the heat and deceptive fiery words of the devil. The devil says we are lost, worthless, runaways, throwaways; we are thieves of the lands, we are broom tails, we are better off wild and untrained. We have no pedigree, no purpose; we are broken, worthless, and hopeless. But do not be fooled by these dishonest thoughts. We are not better off wild and untamed, living in fear and pain. We can overcome this deception and hunger by seeking after the Ultimate Trainer.

When we rest in the Handler's presence, He renews our minds with the goodness we possess. He gives us the opportunity to break free of our generational curses. The Ultimate Trainer gives us purpose, strength, elegance, wisdom, and knowledge. He gives us to hide as tough as armor and a heart mighty like a warrior. When we were thought to have no pedigree, He poured out His grace to make us heirs and joint heirs of His kingdom. We have royal blood flowing through our veins. When we are called wild, weak, and worthless, remember we are more than just a throwaway; we are priceless. We were wild, but now we are worthy.

> And we pray this in order that you may live a life worthy of the Lord and may please him in every way: bearing fruit in every good work, growing in the knowledge of God, being strengthened with all power according to his glorious might so that you may have great endurance and patience.
>
> COLOSSIANS 1:10-11

Be Willing to Lie Down

Whether in life or in horsemanship, when you force something to happen, it often results in resentment. The Ultimate Trainer never teaches by force. Whether we are working with people or horses that conflict with our spirit, we must focus on building up a strong foundation first on respect, trust, love, and patience, just as a right relationship with Jesus Christ displays these attributes.

When training horses, once the relationship has progressed where we have proved that we can be a worthy leader, we can ask our horses progressive questions. We can take our horse-human relationship past infant understanding and move it into adult teachings.

From a horsemanship point of view, a horse rarely lays down. If it does, it's typically no more than an hour to get some deep REM sleep while others in its herd are watching over them. The other time horses lay down is typically right before they die.

When taking on the responsibility of asking a horse to lie down, be educated first to know what you're getting yourself into. If you do not have trust and respect built up first, this will often not be successful.

Just as the Lord doesn't force us to lie down, we shouldn't demand force from a horse. In my faith, the Lord has showed up and showed out in my life. He has proved time and time again that He provides everything I need. He gives me comfort, peace, and contentment. He built me up from infant understanding and progressed me into adult teachings. He moved me from milk to meat. I trust Him with everything, which allows me to willingly lay down.

This is what I'm after when I ask a horse to lay down for me.

We must ask clear questions without forcing the answer. If the horse doesn't understand, we must break down the question into smaller steps to allow the horse to figure out the right answer. We must find ways to constantly offer the right answer with ease. During the process, the handler is responsible for keeping the peace, deflecting frustration, and keeping a clear mind. As the Ultimate Trainer sticks by us until we find the release from pressure, we must stick by our horse until he figures out what the release is; in this case, the willingness to lay down.

Whether in faith or in horsemanship, it's hard to put ourselves in a vulnerable position. Try looking at the situation from another perspective.

Don't focus on the result.
Learn from the journey.
Be present.

We must be willing to walk side by side with our horses. We must go together. Don't forcefully drag him down. Build up your partner's confidence and trust so he wishes to willingly bow. It's not about submission; it's about being in full accord.

To be one mind, one spirit, and be in the same place together mentally (Philippians 2:2).

The Lord doesn't make us lay down. He offers it (Psalm 23).

Once you accept His grace and kindness, all things are possible through Christ Jesus.

For I know my victory is in Jesus.

The horse is made ready for the day of battle, but victory rests with the Lord (Proverbs 21:31).

What Does Your Face Say?

The more sensitive we are to the changes the horse makes and the more we reward him accordingly, the more sensitive the horse can be in his response.

MARTIN BLACK

Like people, horses send a lot of messages with their facial expressions and body language. The positioning of their neck and head, the movement of their ears and eyes, and the tightness around the muzzle are all strong indicators of their state of mind.

If we can apply simple Christian principles to building the right relationship with our horses, we can become more sensitive, softer, and kinder and display Christ-like character not just in our horsemanship but in the arena of life. These Christ-like attributes should be the core reflection of our soul and the fruits we bear:

But the fruit of the Spirit is love, joy, peace, Forbearance, kindness, goodness, faithfulness, gentleness, and self-control.

Against such things, there is no law.

We need to be kinder with our body language when our mouth is shut. Ever had a person or horse flee from you at first sight without saying a word?

Chances are they picked up on what your body was saying. For horses have an unheard language. They do not have to say a word to move one another, show respect for the boss mare, offer a helping mouth scratch, etc.

Just as the Lord has such a powerful unheard language through the Holy Spirit.

Think less, show up, and be present where you are now.

We need to learn to seek the Lord for guidance and answers, not worldly opinions.

Embrace discernment, not the essence of scientific energy.

The word energy is used out of context often and should only be referred to as the quality of motion, much described in going forward.

You must have the absence of judgment but have a view to obtaining spiritual guidance from Jesus, known as discernment. But it starts with humbly laying yourself down, seeking out the truth of Jesus, and the willingness to become aware of His unheard language. He then will bless you with wisdom, leading to understanding. If you're willing to accept the correction and guidance.

> The man without the Spirit does not accept the things that come from the Spirit of God, for they are foolishness to him, and he cannot understand them, because they are spiritually discerned.

> 1 CORINTHIANS 2:14

Faith Comes by Hearing

Let's be real, training horses is rewarding, but it is hard! It doesn't matter if it's on a professional level or caring for retired pasture puffs. They all desire the need for the right relationship. It's up to us whether we offer that and maintain it. Even if we skip out on the time deserved, horses still require a lot of maintenance, money, and space to keep them healthy and happy. When we desire the right relationship that brings us to an undiscovered full potential, it's no different when we truly commit to following the Ultimate Trainer. He knows training us is rewarding, but it is hard, especially since He allows us to have free will and make our own choices. No tricks, no gimmicks, and no micromanaging. He wants us to willingly follow Him. He has a full book of instructions to remind us to stay encouraged.

The Master Horseman waits patiently for us to fully commit instead of skimping out on time needed. He constantly puts in the effort to maintain the right relationship taking us to our full potential. He reminds us that we need to read His Word for ourselves to hear Him. We can only come to faith by hearing the gospel. When we completely trust our Handler, then we have to remind ourselves of our Handler's instructions to instill His truth in our lives. If we are not sensitive to the Spirit that drew us, how can we hear, grow, and understand? How can we hear Him be encouraged? How can we hear Him stay on course? How can we hear Him to keep our peace?

When we get into a position of doubt, fear creeps in and overrides our faith. We must remind ourselves to restore our faith. How do we restore our faith?

By reciting scripture, by playing the Master Horseman's message in our minds when we are paralyzed by fear to mount up on that green horse for the first time, remember fear is a liar. If we put the work in, we have nothing to fear. When we are full of anxiety when entering the arena for a show class, we breathe and remember the words we've heard that are stored in our hearts.

> Consequently, faith comes from hearing the message, and the message is heard through the word of Christ.
>
> ROMANS 10:17

Spur One Another On

To dwell in the most holy of places, we first must be drawn by the Spirit. Then we can be washed clean with pure water. Once we are drawn by the Spirit, our Handler can then lead us to safety and treasures in the barn. Much like when we get ready for a horse show, we must be able to be caught and haltered. Then we can be led into the wash rack to be washed clean, transforming the stained hide into a glistening coat. We can then rest our horse easily in the plush comforts of its stall with endless hay, clean water, electrolytes, and free-choice minerals. All the while, our horse looks like it's ready for the day of battle as we have our horse wrapped in its sleazy Lycra hood to keep its mane and face clean. Our horse's tail is wrapped, padded, and bagged to protect it from being rubbed, fluffed, cut, or tangled. Dependent on the season, it may be decked out under a stable sheet or blanket for ease of grooming, especially at the show grounds. Horse showing may not be everyone's cup of tea. However, it's important to expose our horses and ourselves to different arenas and environments. Horses don't get broke at home. Meaning they need miles and opportunities to grow their confidence. We can't grow if we are in a constant state of comfort. We must push ourselves and our horses to keep faith in uncomfortable situations. We must hold tightly to the hope we have in the Ultimate Trainer, not white knuckle the reins. Allow Master Horseman to redirect your feet when uneasy and spur you on toward love.

> Let us hold unswervingly to the hope we profess, for he who promised is faithful. And let us consider how we may spur one another on toward love and good deeds.

HEBREWS 10:23-24

We Are Not
Promised Tomorrow

A man I know is now a man I once knew. This man was one of the greatest men on earth. He taught me respect, he disciplined me, he showed me the gift of horses, he showed me how to use tools, he showed me how to work on vehicles, he showed me miles of beautiful country, he showed me the joy of dirt roads, he showed me love, and he taught me about Jesus. This man never had to step into my life, as he was always in it. He saved the day numerous times when I was a kid. When my mom passed out on the floor from too many painkillers at age six, I wasn't strong enough to get her up, but he was. He was always a phone call away to swoop in and come to the rescue. When Mom couldn't take me to a horseback riding lesson, he again came in to do so. When my earthly dad left the scene, he was there yet again to offer the guidance of a father. This man I'm referring to was strong and had unforgettable working hands. His staple attire was his jean material Wrangler pearl snap shirt, Wrangler jeans, comfortable boots, and topped off with his favorite straw or felt cowboy hat, dependent on the season. This man was what I described as a perfect cross between John Wayne and Jesus.

This man loved his country by serving in the Air Force. He loved to work and build things. Most of all, this man loved Jesus. This man, at eighty-five years old on November 17, 2016, rededicated his life to Jesus Christ, followed by getting baptized at the Potter's House Church. This was remarkable for my husband and me to see. In this man's final months, I had the pleasure of offering 24/7 hospice care to him for two weeks around Christmas. It was exhausting, amazing, fulfilling, and some of the most cherished memories I will ever have. We prayed, we read scripture, we cried, we laughed, and we talked truth and love. I encouraged him. I reminded him to keep his hope and trust in Jesus through the suffering. Those two weeks of service will never compare to what this man has offered in my life. I can say with confidence I know this man is no longer suffering here on earth. I am confident to say this man knew in his final hours the Lord was calling him home, and he even said so. Even with his failing memory and failing heart, this man cried out to Jesus for forgiveness and kept his faith in Him. This man earned his promotion to heaven to the fullest.

To be absent from the body is to be present with Christ. I'm sure he was greeted at the gates with open arms by all those that loved him, including my mom and dad. This man bared fruit in old age. So who is this amazing man I've rattled on about?

Without further ado, this man was my grandpa, my father, and to my husband, he was Paw. His name was Robert Dean Scrivner. He gained his promotion on February 8, 2022, at age ninety. I'm going to miss this man terribly, but I find comfort and peace knowing in Jesus, his mind and body are now restored. I will see you again, Grandpa. I love you so much. I mean it, and I'm not kidding. I praise the Lord for His wisdom and growth through this tough experience.

I praise the Lord for the guidance of the gift of scripture that was shared. I praise the Lord for my husband, my dearest mentors, and my friends, offering encouragement through this time.

May you be encouraged by these verses just as much as Grandpa was by these specific ones.

THE ROMANS ROAD TO SALVATION

He gives strength to the weary and increases the power of the weak. Even youths grow tired and weary, and young men stumble and fall but those who hope in the LORD will renew their strength.

ISAIAH 40:29-31A

My flesh and my heart may fail,
but God is the strength of my heart
and my portion forever.

PSALM 73:26

For if you live according to the flesh, you will die; but if by the Spirit you put to death the misdeeds of the body, you will live.

ROMANS 8:13

Do not let your hearts be troubled. You believe in God; believe also in me. My Father's house has many rooms; if that were not so, would I have told you that I am going there to prepare a place for you? And if I go and prepare a place for you, I will come back and take you to be with me that you also may be where I am.

JOHN 14:1-3

Not only so, but we also glory in our sufferings, because we know that suffering produces perseverance; perseverance, character; and character, hope. And hope does not put us to shame, because God's love has been poured out into our hearts through the Holy Spirit, who has been given to us.

ROMANS 5:3-5

ABOUT THE AUTHOR

Jessica Shively is a Marine Corps veteran who started an equine facility, Trail of Faith Farms, in eastern North Carolina in 2013. Jessica is originally from Idaho, and her husband, Joshua, is originally from Virginia. They both loved being stationed in North Carolina and decided to permanently reside on the east coast after their military enlistment. Joshua's persistence and encouragement pushed Jessica to fulfill her dreams of working with horses. Jessica's strong faith and dedication have led her to become a full-time trainer in Natural Horsemanship, working with domestic horses and wild mustangs. Jessica is also a PATH International certified instructor and an approved trainer through the Mustang Heritage Foundation and Bureau of Land Management.

The foundation of her training techniques is based on Natural Horsemanship that's taught by world-known professionals such as Pat and Linda Parelli. Her teaching methods are also influenced by Lynn Baber, Paul Daily, Monty Roberts, Ray Hunt, Buck Brannaman, and professional reining trainers like Shawn Flarida and Jesse Chase.

Jessica is a passionate equestrian who strives to bring new ideas to every horse and human relationship. She applies her Christian values in her life as well as in her horse training and therapeutic riding. She has over twenty-five years of experience riding, training, teaching, and working with people with various diagnoses.

Jessica excels at bringing horses and humans together to teach the art of communication, as well as helping them to overcome emotional and physical challenges in the comforts of the barn and arena.

ABOUT TRAIL OF FAITH FARMS

Trail of Faith Farms (TOFF) is a Christian-based equine facility located in Trenton, North Carolina.

TOFF offers beginner thru advanced western lessons (specializing in ranch, reining, and trail), therapeutic riding, mustang gentling, and Natural Horsemanship training. Our mission is to serve all horse enthusiasts, from able-bodied to disabled individuals. We serve children and adults dealing with a wide variety of diagnoses, from PTSD, autism, cerebral palsy, depression, and more. TOFF provides services to active-duty military, veterans, and their families through our Operation No Longer a Number program.

TOFF is a direct source for the Wounded Warrior Battalion on Camp Lejeune and welcomes all veterans seeking equine-assisted therapy or lessons.

TOFF offers diverse activities throughout the year, such as Rodeos, Parelli Natural Horsemanship Clinics, Working Cow Clinics, Trick Riding Clinics, Horsemanship clinics, Trail Obstacle Challenges, and more!

Our goal is to uplift souls and spread the Word of Jesus Christ using horses.

Connect with Jessica @TrailofFaithFarms or visit the Trail of Faith Farms website.